Project Nehemiah

Learn more about this book and its author by visiting our web site:

www.overboardministries.com

ISBN:0983456836
ISBN-13:978-09834568-3-4

Cover design by Innovative Graphics
www.igprodesign.com

This title is available for your favorite eReader.
Visit our web site to choose the format
that's right for you.

All comments or requests for
information should be sent to:
overboard@overboardministries.com

DEDICATION

On December 28th, 1996, I heard two words that almost made me leap for joy and shout "HALLELUJAH" at the top of my lungs. Of course, I was on a stage with about 350 people in the audience, so I restrained myself considerably. Those words were "I do," and they were spoken by my then fiancée, Traci. Part of me wondered if she had any idea what she was saying, but another part of me wanted to make sure she didn't get a chance to reconsider. So I did the only reasonable thing a man would do in my situation — I kissed her and walked off the stage to cheers and relief; she was now my wife.

Fifteen years later and I still shout "HALLELUJAH" when I think of her decision to commit herself first to God, then to me. During these wonderful years of marriage, we've navigated a few average days, a handful of good ones and a mountain-load of great ones. God blessed me with a wife who isn't restrained by what "they" say or isn't concerned with what *can't* be done. She's a dreamer, and her dreams have grown in proportion to her beautiful and active relationship with the Creator. She inspires me to reach higher and further and to trust God more. Together, we have seen Him do much with our feeble efforts deeply rooted in faith.

I dedicate this book to you, my bride, as a meager token of thanks for all the ways you've inspired me to grow. Thank you for your unyielding love, support and faith even when I merited much less. I pray that these principles continue to be evident in our lives and marriage together and that our children's children will know what it means to trust God fully and follow Him in faith. Already He has done far more than we could have imagined, guessed or requested in our wildest dreams, and yet, somehow, I am confident the best is yet to come.

All my love, always.

CONTENTS

	Dedication	iii
	Acknowledgments	ix
	Foreword	xi
	Introduction	xiii
1	Who is Nehemiah?	1
2	Moved to Action	7
3	Powerful Prayers	21
4	Ginormous Dreams	35
5	Honest Assessment	45
6	Who Are Your Friends?	55
7	The Heat and the Hammer	67
8	Finish the Wall	91
9	People Not Projects	103
10	Start Building	111
	About the Author	115
	Who or What is Overboard Books?	117
	Overboard Resources	121
	About the Cover	123
	Project Joseph: Chapter 1 preview	125

TESTIMONIALS

Project Nehemiah touched a place in my heart where many entrepreneurs, like me, struggle. Trusting in God to be part of every aspect of our lives can be a constant struggle that holds many of us back from reaching our full potential, especially when it comes to God-sized dreams. This book provides touching real-life stories, Scripture, humor and practical how-to's to teach us how and why to allow God to be the CEO of our lives. If you have ever had an unfulfilled dream that God has placed on your heart, allow *Project Nehemiah* to rejuvenate and ignite it into reality.

Amber Thiel
Cofounder and CEO of The Healthy Edge
www.getthehealthyedge.com

* * * * *

Joe has done it again! In *Project Joseph,* he offered practical steps to overcoming life's hurts. In *Project Nehemiah,* Joe unpacks a biblical pattern for dreaming big and accomplishing great things for God's glory. The biblical story provides the principles; Joe unpacks them. But he doesn't leave them there. He also surrounds that framework with real-life stories of people doing God-sized things, so the reader can see the principles play out. This book will help dreamers with the step-by-step process to turn their dreams into reality, and it will help practically-minded people expand the size of their dreams.

Kevin Hearne
Pastor, Central Point Community Church

* * * * *

I just finished Joseph Castañeda's most recent book, *Project Nehemiah,* last week. Joe is one of those guys who just resonates with people through captivating stories. This book is challenging, humorous, and compelling. The wisdom in these pages is deep. I know I was challenged to the core of who I am and why I do what I do.

The principles, ideas and strategies in this book will help you navigate to the remarkable life that God has designed for you. Joe's passion is to move people from being spectators in the faith to people of action. *Project Nehemiah* does a wonderful job of inspiring forward progress in the faith. If you have a ginormous dream, *Project Nehemiah* will challenge you to think even bigger, and then wait and see how God shows up. It's practical, it's funny and it will inspire you to live out those God-sized dreams for your life.

Danny Ray
Illusionist and Speaker
www.dannyray.tv

* * * * *

I love *Project Nehemiah.* The parallel with Cherrie and Nehemiah makes great word pictures, and anyone who reads this book will be able to easily understand the concepts. Being an emotional person, I always cry when I read the story of Nehemiah, and I cried equally with Cherrie's story. Yes, one person can make a difference, and that idea is made clear, over and over, in the pages of this book. I think the way the seven steps of kingdom-building are presented is a portrayal of exactly what God would want each of His children to do in their service to Him. Thanks for another great book, Joe. Your Mom loves and appreciates you.

Jeanne Castañeda
Author's mom

ACKNOWLEDGMENTS

I have four unfinished books sitting on my computer's desktop. The fact that you are holding this volume is a testament to a number of people, people who worked hard to keep me on task and to proof, reproof and re-reproof every word of this book. Of course, first on that list is *my amazing wife, Traci*. She is the heart and soul of our Nehemiah-like projects, and without her I would have five unfinished books on my computer's desktop.

Next in line is another one of Overboard Ministries' *awesome editors, Ellen Kersey*. Ellen has been a great friend and support all of our years in Salem, and her friendship and support grew even more during this project. Thank you, Ellen, for making my writing better, and, for teaching me, carefully, how to use, but not abuse, each, and every, comma, in this book.

I'm also indebted to my *friend and editor, Brenda Noland*. Brenda edited my first book, *Project Joseph,* and was gracious enough to give this book one last review before we sent it off to the printers.

I would also like to thank *my pastor, Tim Baker,* for his incredible support. He has given me time to write, offered insights into biblical passages, and been a sounding board any time I popped into his office. He is gracious, even when I text his phone during staff meetings just to make the phone ring; or when I crack jokes about his lack of a Facebook page (which has since been remedied). Thanks, Sahib, for your support and friendship.

And finally, I thank *my loving Lord and Savior, Jesus Christ* for the privilege of service. I pray that this book pleases you first, and that you will entrust me with many more wall-building projects in the future. Thank you, God, for your ever-present grace.

FOREWORD

I'm a dad. As a dad, one of the things you learn is that your kids like to make you "stuff." You quickly learn that you can't keep all of the "stuff" they make. Some of the "art" quickly finds its way to the recycle bin, while other creations are "refrigerator-worthy." Recently my kids have been into knitting. The other day I came home and saw a scarf that looked like it had been bought from a store, but it turned out my kids had made it. I was proud and blown away!

This is going to sound a little weird, but I felt that same feeling while reading this book. Joe has been a good friend for a number of years, so, when he asked me to read this book, I was more than happy to do it. I figured I'd be looking for spelling errors and giving opinions about the illustrations he chose, but, not far into the first chapter, I found myself proud and blown away! I've always admired Joe as a friend and mentor in the ministry, but Project Nehemiah has far exceeded my expectations (and after his last book, my expectations were pretty high).

I went from reading a book for a friend to being challenged by God to dream big dreams for the Kingdom! I stopped looking for misspelled words and began to search my soul for the things that I've allowed to creep in and hinder the work of God in my life. I began putting into practice the biblical principles that Joe has drawn from the life of Nehemiah. This book has inspired and challenged me like no other book has done in a long time.

Although this book is based on the life of Nehemiah, it's not a commentary on the book of Nehemiah. Joe pulls out key principles from Nehemiah's journey that each of us who are striving to follow Christ wholeheartedly can put into practice. All the while he tells personal stories, along with stories of other modern-day Nehemiahs who are at work "building walls" for God's glory here and around the world.

Joe writes in a way that is humorous, engaging, humble and very practical. Some books have so much theory that it's hard to put anything into action. Joe has designed *Project Nehemiah* with action steps in mind. The end of each chapter has a series of questions designed to help us engage God's dream for our lives. If you're willing to put in some time and effort, this is a powerful tool that God will use to inspire and move you into significant Kingdom work…whether that's around the globe or around the block!

Books are a lot like artwork from kids. Some books quickly find their way to a donation pile, while others sit on our shelves for years and are referenced often. *Project Nehemiah* will most certainly be staying in my collection and will continue to be a blessing to me, as I'm sure it will be to you!

Andy Hartfield
Youth Pastor, Colorado Springs
AIM Missionary appointee, Tanzania, Africa

INTRODUCTION

About nine months ago, I had the joy of finishing my first book, *Project Joseph*. It was written to help people deal with pain in their lives by seeing key principles from the life of Joseph from the book of Genesis. *Project Joseph* struck a nerve, and the response from readers has been an incredibly humbling testament to God's work in my life and in the lives of those who are turning to Him for healing.

I believe God helped me unpack the message of *Project Joseph,* and as He did, He gave me outlines for several other books in the same vein. I hate the term "self-help" when it applies to Christian literature because "self" is usually what gets us *into* trouble, not *out of* trouble. It's reliance on our own character and strength that leaves us worse off than before. It's self that is at the heart of so many of our sins before a holy God.

So, while trying to avoid the "self-help" genre, I still wanted to write a book that practically outlined God's path for healing. If pain and heartache were worked on in accordance with God's Word and in dependence on His power, a believer could experience life-long healing from heartache, even if that heartache was years old. Of course, this type of healing requires hard work, discipline, focused prayer and grace that must come from God, but it must be sought and developed.

Far from self-help, however, we become a helpless-self, working with God to see open wounds mended and mended wounds healed. From that concept emerged *Project Joseph,* the first of several books of this nature in what has become known as "The Life Improvement Series."

The second book, the one you are now holding, was a natural follow-up to the first. If *Project Joseph* is about how God wants to help you heal from your past pain, *Project Nehemiah* is about how God wants you to plan your future. Just as I am confident that God's Word gives us practical instruction and clear commands for mending our brokenness, it also gives us clear commands that teach us to live in total faith today, while still dreaming big God-sized dreams for the future.

Project Nehemiah seeks to resolve the tension many believers face: how do I trust God for everything; how do I trust His plan for the future, but still make plans and still have dreams about what's next in my life? Not only is it possible to live successfully in that tension, but God yearns for His children to trust Him fully, while dreaming wildly about what He could do through them as they trust Him even more. It sounds circular. It *is* circular. But it's a divine circular, and it works. The Old Testament story of Nehemiah is proof.

As you embark on this journey of learning to dream about a future that is God-focused, God-driven and God-sized, you will journey with Nehemiah, a rather unremarkable person who lived a truly remarkable life. The seven principles of planning for the future according to God's design, as seen in Nehemiah's life, are transferable to you. Understanding them isn't difficult, but applying them will require a deep dependence on God, not on self. Again, it's a helpless-self working with God to do what only God can ultimately do.

To help further illustrate the principles from Nehemiah's life, I want to share with you the story of another person who, from the outside, looks fairly unremarkable, but who is living out a remarkable life today. Her story of how God is moving and working in and through her further illustrates the key truths we'll unpack from the story of Nehemiah. In each chapter of *Project Nehemiah* I will share more and more of her story.

Who is she?

Let me introduce you to my friend Cherrie, a modern-day Nehemiah. You see, 18 months before I started writing this book, Cherrie was living a good life. She was celebrating twenty three years of marriage with her loving husband, Rick. She owned a small and successful photography studio, had the joy of having her two oldest kids in a Christian university, and her youngest was just a few months from finishing high school. She and her husband loved God. They had a beautiful home in an idyllic setting on the outskirts of our town. She was happy and thankful to God for her life and for the comforts He had given her.

That was 18 months ago.

When I conducted my three-hour interview with Cherrie, she was sitting on the floor in her living room holding a beautiful Ethiopian baby named Juddah. She wore a necklace with a pendant in the shape of the continent of Africa. I noticed her iPhone had a custom-made skin with a map of Ethiopia highlighting each of the major cities of that country. She had a tattoo on her right wrist in a foreign language, which she told me was a reference to Psalm 121:1-2 in Amharic (one of many languages spoken in the region). At one point during our interview, in this beautiful home overlooking the beautiful valley below, she looked at me, with tears in her eyes, and said, "I want to live in the sewer of Korah; physically one of the most disgusting places I've ever seen, but full of such beautiful people."

A lot can happen in 18 months.

In the fall of 2009, Cherrie attended a presentation by Invisible Children, a group that works to help free children who have been forced into slavery or turned into soldiers — children as young as six or seven. After a video presentation, a young man spoke about the terror of living in a nation where children were forced to become cold-blooded killers. He spoke of the horrors of being forced to murder his own brother and watching his brother's body be mutilated by those seeking to control these children through fear. He broke people's hearts and tried to convey the need for those with resources to help organizations like Invisible Children save children.

God planted a seed in Cherrie's heart.

In February of 2010, just a few months after the presentation by Invisible Children, Cherrie got a call from a good friend who was inviting her to Africa. This trip, less than two weeks long, would give them a chance to travel with an organization called Visiting Orphans, giving them exposure to the needs of children in Uganda and Ethiopia. Cherrie asked her husband Rick, they prayed and felt confirmation from God, and plans were made for an April departure.

Cherrie and her team spent the first week of their trip in Uganda. While there, she was exposed to first-hand experiences of a man who had escaped the LRA (Lord's Resistance Army) as a teenager. Their stories of the horrific nature of war and genocide started growing the seed that God had already planted in her heart. Cherrie was becoming certain that God wanted her to do *something* to help organizations like Invisible Children or Visiting Orphans to free kids from being soldiers. When she was preparing to leave Uganda, she felt an overwhelming need to give money to Pastor Isaac, a man already steeped in the rescue work.

In the middle of the day, Uganda time, Cherrie called home and awoke her husband in the middle of the night, Oregon time. The essence of her call was simple: "Rick, I need you to deposit a large sum of money into my account. God wants me to give it away." Rick was a little groggy, but snapped to when he heard the request. He asked a few questions to which Cherrie replied, "I just need you to trust me." And he did. Rick didn't go back to sleep until the task was finished.

Once Cherrie knew the funds — thousands of dollars — were in her account, she headed to the bank to withdraw the money to give to Pastor Isaac, who was unaware of her plans. It was here that Cherrie's plans stalled when she discovered that she couldn't take out more than $300 at any one Ugandan bank. In fact, if she withdrew $300 from one bank, none of the other banks would allow her to access more. She had a limit, so the remaining cash couldn't be accessed.

Because her team was leaving for Ethiopia, Cherrie was forced to wonder what God was doing. She knew God wanted her to act and felt confident that He had given her this dollar figure. Her husband Rick, a godly man himself, trusted his wife's relationship with God and her sensing of God's call to action. Yet Cherrie left Uganda feeling frustrated that God's clear direction suddenly seemed hazy and uncertain.

In Ethiopia, the Visiting Orphans tour group kept the team busy. Sometimes, they would play soccer with street kids and visit schools, and at other times they would visit two or three orphanages a day, seeing the full scope of the need in this impoverished nation. On the eve of her departure from Ethiopia, she was still wondering how God was going to allow her to use the remaining funds in her account to bless Pastor Isaac and the work in Uganda.

Then something unexpected happened: a volcano erupted in Iceland. The volcanic ash spewed across much of Europe, and, since their return flight went through Amsterdam, the Visiting Orphans team was grounded in Ethiopia for the next two weeks. During this stay, the seed God planted in her heart a few months before during a seminar on child-soldiers, the one that was cultivated further in Uganda, finally took root in Ethiopia, and Cherrie was changed.

Her team continued to work in Ethiopia for the extra fourteen days. One night, after spending two hours in a downpour delivering food and helping the needy, she was in the guest house where they stayed, listening to a young man named Sammy share his story. Sammy was from Korah. In my interview with Cherrie, she called Korah "the pit of hell," a "sewer" and "physically, the most disgusting place I've ever been." She's quick to say, "The people are beautiful, and their resilient faith and strong perseverance are remarkable and inspiring." It's just that Korah stinks.

You see, Korah is the location of the capital city's dump. It is home to a 50-year-old leprosy hospital, a place where lepers can be seen dragging themselves down the street. It's a dead end town. People who are born there are essentially sentenced to a life of poverty and misery. More than 130,000 people call Korah home, and many of them couldn't survive if they didn't have the city dump from which to get their food. The air is foul. Ashes from the constant burning of the garbage give people's faces a ghostly film. This was Sammy's home.

Cherrie heard how Sammy's dad had been shot in the face and then pushed off a cliff and left for dead — by his own brothers! You see, Sammy's father had contracted leprosy, and the shame of that disease drove Sammy's grandfather to command his other children to kill Sammy's dad. Sammy's uncles had been the ones to shoot his father in the face and push him off the cliff!

Cherrie then heard how his father was rescued by some "good Samaritans" and taken to the leprosy hospital, and how his dad met his mom. With each piece of Sammy's story, Cherrie started to see what God was doing in bringing her to Africa. Sammy had been living in the dump from the earliest age, and by four was a "lifer." Even as a young boy, he was sickened by having to watch his mom and grandmother forage each day at the dump.

At age 14, while most of his friends were rescued and taken to school by various state and humanitarian programs, Sammy wasn't granted that help; instead, he was forced to continue his life in the dump. But God sent the first-ever Young Life team to Korah that year, and Sammy discovered a God who loved him more than anything. Despite his awful living conditions, Sammy found hope, and by age 15 he had determined he was going to be used by God to reach the children of the dump.

So Sammy opened a bank account and began saving money to build a home for children who called the dump "home." Now 24, Sammy was still working with children in the dump, still preparing for his dream. Cherrie asked him to share his plans, and he pulled out a piece of paper to draw everything out — building plans, budgets, timelines. Nine years of waiting hadn't dulled his dream; they had refined it and strengthened his resolved to trust God to bring along a Nehemiah to see it fulfilled.

Cherrie's heart was overwhelmed. In that moment of total clarity, she realized that God had used the testimony of a child soldier in the fall of 2009 to soften her heart to say "yes" to a tour of orphanages in February of 2010. She understood that the pastor in Uganda was used by God to get her to acquire funds, not for his ministry, but for a house in Ethiopia. God used the banking limits in Uganda to keep her from meeting one need because He wanted her to meet another.

In that moment, she realized that God had used a volcano in Iceland to help delay her return to the U.S., so her heart might be broken by a young man named Sammy. What Cherrie saw in that flash of divine understanding was that God wanted more than her money — He wanted her life. Today Cherrie is part of a team of people who are building homes, who are bringing hope, help and healing to people living in a dump.

As you read *Project Nehemiah* I hope you will be challenged by God's Word as it applies to your life. And as you think about its application to you, I hope Cherrie's story will help you realize that God's plans are bigger than you or I could ever imagine. Neither the biblical Nehemiah nor his modern-day counterpart, Cherrie, were "superstars" in their faith. They didn't possess more talent, more money or more opportunity than others of their time. Instead, they embodied a lifestyle seen in seven transferable principles. If you live these principles out in your life, you too can join the remarkable story: building hope where walls lay in ruin and where garbage dumps are a source for food. God isn't looking for stars in his next reality show, "Heaven's Got Talent" — He's looking for Nehemiahs and Cherries, people who will live life according to His Word.

Over the last few years of our lives, my wife and I have adopted Ephesians 3:20 as the verse we want to embody in our marriage. We want it to permeate what we do as a couple and to play out in each part of our lives — parenting, ministry, business, writing, coaching, etc. You might be familiar with the words of this verse, but check it out in The Message translation:

> *"God can do anything, you know — far more than you could ever imagine or guess or request in your wildest dreams!"* (Ephesians 3:20)

God has big plans for you. As you read *Project Nehemiah,* I pray that you will choose to follow the principles of God's Word to see those plans unfold in your life. Like Peter, jumping overboard to walk on water — to do the impossible! — with God can be a scary venture, but one that will change your life forever.

May God bless you as you read and apply the principles of His Word as represented in the pages of this book.

"After such an introduction, I can hardly wait to see what I'm going to say."
Evelyn Anderson

Chapter One
Who is Nehemiah?

I've never been fond of introductions. As a camp speaker, I usually prefer the musicians to finish their last song and just walk off stage while I walk up. In other venues, I appreciate an emcee who simply states, "And now it's time for our guest speaker" and then invites me to get into the message. I don't mind a good friend who shares a story about our friendship or a story that might help validate what I'm about to say, but generally speaking, I like to get going. Introductions can be awkward, and, if done poorly, can distract from the message the speaker is about to bring.

Introducing Joe

A few years ago I was speaking at a Bible conference for a local Christian school. It was a Monday night, and I was sitting in the front row as the small auditorium was filling up with parents and students, maybe 250-300 in attendance. Four days before, I had received a call from one of the school's teachers, a good friend, who asked if I could be available in a pinch. Apparently, the school had booked another speaker who had just called and had to cancel his engagement due to personal reasons. My friend told me they were checking other options, but wanted to know if I was free.

I checked my schedule, and wouldn't you know it — I was free! The only other date I had booked that year was nine months away, so I had a small window of opportunity (just 270 days!) to squeeze in this week of Bible conference if they needed me. Late

Saturday afternoon I received a confirmation call from the coordinator of the conference, and, indeed, I was on.

So there I sat, Monday night at 6:50, meeting the conference coordinator for the first time. She was a kind woman who asked me lots of questions as she was about to introduce me. She asked me about my previous speaking engagements, and I shared that my wife and I had done some work in Canada with a small group of students, and we had just recently returned from a couple of weeks of ministry in Spain, where I had spoken at a summer camp for missionary kids. She asked about my wife, my family (we had just one child at the time) and the ministry I had here in Salem, where we had been serving for just over one year.

Then she thanked me for being willing to step in and casually mentioned the name of the speaker whose circumstances had forced him to turn down this opportunity. My jaw dropped. I hadn't heard his name up to this point, and suddenly I realized why they were trying so hard to get *someone* to speak. This man's name was synonymous with youth ministry. This guy was a "guru." This guy was a household name. People knew who he was — none of them would know who I was.

I had a sick feeling in the pit of my stomach and contemplated faking a heart attack to see if I could get out of it. Too late. The woman who had asked me all the questions was already welcoming the crowd and introducing me. She said, "We are so excited about this year's speaker [translation: He's not who you thought he was...in fact, he's the only guy who happened to be free at the last minute. Please be kind]. He's a local youth pastor [translation: That means he's hip, and cool, so you kids should like him] who has been pastoring for six years [translation: That means he's still pretty young, but has a little experience. You parents should like him]. He's an international speaker [translation: I scraped the bottom of the barrel to come up with something to make him sound interesting], who has spoken in places like Canada, Spain and Mexico [translation: Maybe if he sounds like he's travelled to interesting places, he'll have good stories?]. Please give a warm welcome to Pastor Joe Castañeda [translation: I hope he doesn't get me fired]."

While she was talking, I started looking around. Who is she talking about? "International speaker?" Wow, the guy she's talking about sure sounds interesting. Then when her intro was over, and she said my name, I knew everyone was in trouble. And with that the Bible conference was launched.

Introducing Nehemiah

We don't have to worry about awkward introductions at the beginning of Nehemiah. In fact, Nehemiah simply states, "My dad is Hacaliah, and this is my story." He isn't introduced as an "international builder" or a "hip young veteran of wall restoration projects." He doesn't mention his schooling abroad or his previous business or construction experience.

We know so little about this man. At the end of chapter one, he tells us his occupation — cupbearer to the king — but he still has revealed next to nothing about his family, his heritage or his credentials for what's about to take place. That's part of what makes the story of Nehemiah (and so many others in the Bible) so interesting. God used an ordinary and somewhat unremarkable man to complete a task that was anything but plain, anything but average.

I can imagine my poor friend having to introduce Nehemiah at some conference. She would ask him about his building experience, and he might mention a small shed he once helped build. She might ask about his family, and Nehemiah would talk about his dad and his brother, but that's really all he'd say. Finally, she'd wonder if he had travelled abroad, and he would casually mention being displaced from Israel and being brought to Babylon during the dispersion, but not much else. Not much would have set poor Nehemiah apart from any other Jew of his day. Armed with next to no information, our conference coordinator would do everything she could to make Nehemiah sound well-travelled, full of interesting stories and experiences.

It's important to note that the man God chose for the task of rebuilding the walls of Jerusalem was not the priest, the pastor or the certified counselor. The man was a cupbearer. He was a man of the work-force. Though known personally by the king, he was not indispensable. The king eventually would allow him to leave his job for over three months! God certainly sets aside some people for unique and specific professions in His plan. (Ezra, the priest, was a key man used to help rebuild the temple during Nehemiah's day.) But often God looks for and calls His faithful children in *any profession*, as long as they are willing to step out and trust Him in all they do.

That was the case for Nehemiah. His credentials didn't necessarily qualify him for the task at hand, but his heart for God and his desire to see God's name and glory magnified — instead of his own — make him God's top candidate for the job. In the same way, you may not see your vocation as qualifying you for ministry to the King, but God isn't looking at your vocation. He is looking at your heart. He is looking at your life for patterns of obedience to His Word and dependence on His Spirit. He will supply all you need for every task He has given you. All He asks you to do is trust Him with the details.

God's call on His children throughout the Bible lies far outside the realm of any particular vocation or age or gender. In 1 Samuel 16, He called a 13-year-old shepherd boy named David to be a king. In Exodus 3, God called an 80-year-old ex-prince to lead His people to the Promised Land. Matthew was a no-name accountant and dishonest tax collector before God called him to a higher service in Matthew 2. Ruth was a foreigner, a widow and a beggar who collected leftover grain in a field before being called by God to be King David's grandmother and one of just three women mentioned in the genealogy of Jesus Himself! Peter, James and John were fishermen called to drop their nets and begin their work as evangelists in Mark 1. Lydia was a merchant who sold fine linen when, in Acts 16, she was set apart to help the Apostle Paul in the spread of the Gospel. Gideon was a farmer. Amos sheared sheep and tended figs. Esther was a hottie and a beauty queen. Jesus Himself was a carpenter. In each case, their vocations were different, but one quality remained constant: these ordinary people did extraordinary acts of service when they depended on God to work out His plan through them.

As you continue through this book, I hope you won't let your pedigree — your past accomplishments as a parent, your grades as a student, your trophies as an athlete, your savvy as a businessman, your credentials as an inventor, your influence as a teacher, your status as a homeless woman, your condition as an addict, your "success" as a pastor or anything else! — hinder you in any way from hearing the clear leading of God through the story of Nehemiah. It's not about you and who you are or what you've done, but, as Nehemiah shows us time and time again, it's about God and who He is and what He can do through you.

Introducing Cherrie

Cherrie is a modern-day Nehemiah. (By the way, this is a good time to remind you that if you haven't read the introduction yet, you should go back and do that now, or the rest of Cherrie's story won't make much sense to you.) She is a talented photographer, but that's not why God used her, even though He has used her pictures to help people see and understand the heartbreak that exists in Korah. Cherrie is a great mom who loves her kids, but that's not why God has used her, even though He has repeatedly used her mothering gifts and skills to nurture so many orphans. Cherrie is an awesome wife, a great cook and an incredible hostess. All are commendable qualities, yet none of them explain why God is using her to change lives in Korah.

Cherrie is deeply devoted to God and to loving people as He does. She is trying to live out the two most important commandments as stated by Jesus:

> *"'The most important one [commandment],' answered Jesus, 'is this: "Hear, O Israel, the Lord our God, the Lord is one. Love the Lord your God with all your heart and with all your soul and with all your mind and with all your strength." The second is this: "Love your neighbor as yourself." There is no commandment greater than these.'"* (Mark 12:29-31)

Love God; love others. As you will see in her story and in Nehemiah's it's all about loving God and loving others. It's not about your education or training or ministry experience or family heritage. It's not about you being old or young or male or female. God wants to use ordinary people who love Him and love others to do extraordinary acts of service, acts like building a wall to protect a city or building a house to take care of children who live in a dump.

Introducing [your name here]

I don't know how you would be introduced at our next Overboard Ministries' conference. Maybe you really are an "international speaker" or a "pioneer in your field of expertise," but the question before you right now has nothing to do with what you've done. The real question before you right now is this: "Will you trust God to work out His amazing plan in your life?" You and I don't bring much to the table that will impress God at any level. Like Nehemiah or Cherrie, it's *you* God wants, not your past, not your accomplishments, not your fame or fortune.

As you prepare to navigate the principles of Nehemiah's life, will you start by coming to God with an openness to trust His leading in your life? The journey to an extraordinary life begins when we let Him take the wheel!

"Today is your day! Your mountain is waiting...
so get on your way!"
Dr. Seuss

Chapter Two
Moved to Action

"Are they going to die?"

That was the question my 6-year-old son asked me that cold December night after we had fed homeless men and women under a bridge here in our city. He had been miserable all evening, as temperatures were well below 20 degrees. Our youth group ended up feeding only about 30 people, as the excessively cold weather drove our homeless population to look for shelter somewhere warm.

When AJ was in bed that night, he called me into his room, and with tears in his eyes, he asked if the people were going to be safe. We talked a bit about their condition, about some of the resources available to help them and about why God wants us to regularly do what we can. I tucked him in for the second time and left his room.

Three minutes later he called me again, and, truthfully, I was a bit irritated. I walked back, ready to chastise him for his unwillingness to go to sleep, when I realized he was still teary-eyed about the night's events. When I moved toward his bed, he asked, "Dad, can I celebrate my seventh birthday under the bridge with the the homeless people? I would like to do a big barbecue, serve chips and pop and even have a cake to cut up. Would that be okay?"

Now I was the one who was teary-eyed, but I was also ecstatic and humbled by his tenderness. Even though his birthday was still six months away, he persisted in his request and made plans throughout the winter and spring. When June 19th rolled around, our family was armed with a barbecue, over 150 hamburger patties and hot dogs, hundreds of buns and individual bags of chips, along with two large coolers full of ice-cold carbonated goodness. My mom and dad, my sister and her family and several family friends showed up to help serve. And yes, we had twelve dozen cupcakes iced in blue — the color AJ chose.

As we served dinner to over one hundred people under the bridge that evening, they kept asking, "What's the occasion? Why are you guys here tonight?" With a fatherly pride and an occasional joyful tear, I pointed to my son — who was handing out drinks and cupcakes at the end of our little service line — and said, "That little boy down there wanted to celebrate his birthday with you today." People were speechless. They were grateful. They were touched by his act of kindness. They wanted to know what moved a little 7-year-old boy to choose to party with homeless people.

Nehemiah's Movement

The first principle of *Project Nehemiah* is this: allow God to move your heart to action. My son AJ had served a dinner under the bridge on a cold December night and through that had been sensitive to God's leading to act further. In the same way, Nehemiah's heart was moved when his brother came to town and gave him this report: *"Those who survived the exile and are back in the province are in great trouble and disgrace. The wall of Jerusalem is broken down, and its gates have been burned with fire"* (Nehemiah 1:3).

When Nehemiah heard what was happening to God's people and to the capital city of their land, *"[he] sat down and wept."* In fact, the text goes on to say that he *"mourned and fasted and prayed before the God of heaven..."* for several days! Nehemiah's heart was broken. Just as AJ had been moved to tears by the events of one December dinner served outside under a bridge in below-freezing conditions, Nehemiah's heart was moved by the displacement of God's people, the brokenness of their city and their humiliation, which ultimately reflected on their God. He wept. He mourned. He fasted. He was moved.

Before we can step into the extraordinary life that I believe God wants each of His children to live, we must first let our hearts be moved by the very things and people that move the heart of God. People in circumstances like these:

- Homeless people who are hungry and cold.
- Displaced people who are in great peril and distress.
- People in other countries who don't have access to clean drinking water.
- Unwed teen moms who feel like nobody loves them or will support them in their parenting.
- An elderly neighbor who can't shovel the snow off his own sidewalk.

You see, it's not the magnitude of the service or activity that makes it extraordinary — it's the movement of the individual as the hands and feet of God that distinguishes their actions as extraordinary. Nehemiah's actions weren't amazing because he built a wall in record time (which is incredible on its own merit). His actions were amazing because he broke through the norm. He broke through ordinary things when others wouldn't.

Redefining Extraordinary

Webster's online dictionary defines ordinary this way: "With no special or distinctive features. Normal." We live in a world that is constantly trying to redefine "ordinary" as something more than it is. For example, in our kids' school, GPAs have been shifted in an attempt to make "normal" more significant. Back in the day, 75% was a solid "C," and "C" was considered average. A child who earned an "A" or a "B" on a report card was doing above-average work. Today, in some of our children's classes,

81-100% is an "A," 65-80 is a "B," and in order to fail, a student has to achieve 25% or less. In other words, 65% or higher is now considered extraordinary — above average.

I'm not making a case for one grading system being superior to another — the merits of the new system may well benefit the students in the school. However, I do think the new system illustrates a cultural shift that tries to make "normal" seem special. We live in a society where you can miss 35 questions out of 100 and be considered top of the class. We're celebrating ordinary.

And that's the problem, because ordinary *is* easy. Normal doesn't require any extra effort on our part. Ordinary doesn't need us to be moved to action. Ordinary is what happens every day when the cold and hungry homeless people of our town go another day without food. Ordinary is the unwed teen mom who goes to school and talks to no one because other students can't relate, or don't want to try. Ordinary is one billion people every day going without clean water to drink. Those things are normal and ordinary. Those things happen every day, in almost every part of the world.

What isn't ordinary or normal is when people, moved by the heart of God, step out and try to do something about the problems or injustices they see in the world. It's not that giving $1.50/day is necessarily that difficult (although in some circumstances it certainly could be!). It's that giving $1.50/day is extraordinary when people, moved by the heart of God, give up a latte twice a week to make sure a child in Rwanda can have food, medical supplies, an education and a chance to break out of the cycle of child-soldiers through groups like Africa New Life Ministries.

Extraordinary is a family of five who gives up a week of vacation at Disneyland and spends the money on building houses for desperate people in a border town in Mexico. It is truly extraordinary when a 7-year-old boy chooses to celebrate his birthday by feeding over 100 homeless people with hamburgers and hot dogs. In one sense, we can't compare adopting a child in Rwanda with building a house in Mexico or with feeding 100 homeless people in Salem, Oregon. On the other hand, when God moves in hearts, a common thread is evident in each of those events — they are well outside of what is considered "normal." They are extraordinary events!

Sensitivity to God

Being moved to action isn't ordinary. First, it requires us to have a sensitivity to God. It's not enough to claim a faith in Him; we must put that faith into practice with keen sensitivity to His Word, to His Spirit and to the conscience He has placed in each of us.

Sensitivity to the Word

James, one of four half-brothers of Jesus, addresses this issue head-on in his book. In James 1:27, he writes, "*Religion that God our Father accepts as pure and faultless is this: to look after orphans and widows in their distress and to keep oneself from being polluted by the world.*" Was this command just a cultural norm — to take care of widows or orphans? No! In fact, when the church got its start in the book of Acts, the first significant trouble that arose among the people involved the care of widows (Acts 6:1). If caring for widows had been normal and easy, the question wouldn't have come up.

But throughout Scripture, God has commanded His children to care for widows and orphans and those in need. He has rebuked and punished people when they failed in this task. Amos 1:13 speaks of the sin of Ammon in killing the unborn. Later, in Amos 2:6-7, God chastises Israel for engaging in slavery, taking advantage of the needy, trampling on the poor and denying justice to the oppressed. In Micah 3:1-2, God promises punishment to leaders who pervert justice and metaphorically "*rip the flesh off those in need.*" In Obadiah 12, God rebukes Edom for watching while others were taken into slavery and for rejoicing in the trouble of others. Not only does God condemn those who commit the sin, but He condemns those who sit by and do nothing.

All of these people stand in judgment because God's Word was clear: they were living in disobedience. God had given laws such as in Leviticus 19:9-10, where He instructed the Israelites to leave food for the poor during the harvest. In chapter 19:13-14, God gave clear laws about dealing honestly with neighbors, paying wages to workers and being sure not to bring harm to those with disabilities. And one verse later in 19:15, God demanded that justice be impartial — not a respecter of a person's pocketbook.

When we look back at the accounts of forthcoming punishment in Amos, Micah and Obadiah, we realize that the punishment was coming as a direct result of clear disobedience to God's Word. Those of us who wish to step out and be something more, to be a part of something remarkable, must choose first to be sensitive to God and His Word. We cannot claim to be doing His work when we aren't living according to His Word.

I've worked full-time with students for over 16 years. During that time I've often come across students who want to "light their campus on fire for God," but don't want to obey their parents when they're told to clean their room or be home by 9 p.m. The problem is that I can't find a command in God's Word that says, "Lighteth thy campus with a holy fire that shineth brighteth", but I can find several that say, *"Honor your father and mother"* and *"Obey your parents in the Lord."* If we want to be used by God to do the extraordinary, we must first be willing to be moved to obey His Word.

Sensitivity to the Spirit

Most young believers start their walks with God by learning to read and understand His book. It is concrete and tangible, and, it's a great place to start. But as we mature in our relationship with God, we must learn to grow in our sensitivity to His leading through the Holy Spirit, who takes up residence in our lives. The Spirit works in connection with the Word of God to lead us directly and to move us to action.

While I'm always leery of someone who says he "felt moved by the Spirit of God to do such and such" and that "such and such" is in contrast to the Word of God, I'm also leery of anyone who wants to obey the Word of God without the help of the Spirit of God. Paul writes in 1 Corinthians 2:

> *"The Spirit searches all things, even the deep things of God… In the same way no one knows the thoughts of God except the Spirit of God. We have not received the spirit of the world but the Spirit who is from God, that we may understand what God has freely given us…The man without the Spirit does not accept the things that come from the Spirit of God…"* (1 Corinthians 2:10-14)

Being extraordinary requires a sensitivity to God's Word and to God's Spirit, who helps us understand and implement the truths of the Word. Nehemiah was moved by the dispersion and trial of God's people, but He also clung to the great promises of God's Word. In his prayer in Nehemiah 1:8-10, he shows incredible spiritual sensitivity and understanding of God's eternal truths. I'm confident God's Spirit was active in Nehemiah's understanding of Scripture, and this was part of what moved him to take action!

> *"Remember the instruction you gave your servant Moses, saying, 'If you are unfaithful, I will scatter you among the nations, but if you return to me and obey my commands, then even if your exiled people are at the farthest horizon, I will gather them from there and bring them to the place I have chosen as a dwelling for my Name.' They are your servants and your people, whom you redeemed by your great strength and your mighty hand."* (Nehemiah 1:8-10)

I'm reminded of Cherrie's story. While she listened to the message of Pastor Isaac and heard his heart for reaching children of the war, the Spirit prompted her to take out a significant sum of money to give to God's work. At the time, Cherrie thought it would be used for Pastor Isaac's ministry, but God wanted to have that money ready for another gift — another divine appointment He had already scheduled for Cherrie. Cherrie didn't need to know the details; she just needed to know the Spirit of God and obey His leading. And she did.

Sensitivity to Our Consciences

Finally, we must remember to be moved by the conscience that God has given each of us. Romans 2:14-15 makes it clear that God has given us consciences as guides for action. Clearly, because our consciences can become hardened and seared, we are never instructed to act solely on the guidance of our consciences, but neither are we commanded to ignore them.

In fact, in Romans 14, Paul went on to explain the importance of not violating our God-give conscience. Check out what he wrote in verses two and three:

> *"One man's faith allows him to eat everything, but another man, whose faith is weak, eats only vegetables. The man who eats everything must not look down on him who does not, and the man who does not eat everything must not condemn the man who does, for God has accepted him."* (Romans 14:2-3)

Paul points out that it is possible for two people to have two different opinions about matters not directly addressed in Scripture. These two godly believers could both be fully convinced they were right about a particular matter, and Paul says they are both right before God. Paul's instruction is that neither person can force his conscience on the other, because it is simply a matter between that man and his relationship to God.

In Paul's day, this food thing was a pretty significant dilemma for young believers in Christ. Many of them had been saved out of lifestyles that included idolatry and pagan worship. So when it was time to go to the market, these believers would never buy meat that had been sacrificed to a pagan god. Their consciences wouldn't allow it. However, other believers couldn't have cared less who the meat was offered to. Without hesitation, they took advantage of the cheaper prices (since the meat was already semi-cooked in the sacrifice, it was offered at a discount price) and rejoiced to have good meat at a lower cost. Their consciences weren't bothered at all.

Basically, Paul ends up telling them, "Hey, you're both right!" The Bible didn't address the problem specifically, so Paul says, "Just make sure you don't try to impose your conscience on someone else."

God's Word says, "Don't murder," so we can clearly teach and admonish believers not to murder. However, God's Word doesn't give us direct instruction about buying cheap meat in a pagan marketplace, so in such situations our consciences, shaped by the Word and by the Spirit, are there to guide us.

At the end of chapter 14, Paul summarizes this issue: "*Let us therefore make every effort to do what leads to peace and to mutual edification. Do not destroy the work of God for the sake of food*" (Romans 14:19). In other words, obey your conscience in these questionable matters and remember to "*keep [the matter] between yourself and God*" (Romans 14:22).

The point is this: sometimes our consciences move us to action, and we must respond when God speaks through our built-in right-and-wrong-o-meters. I wonder how many other people in Nehemiah's day had seen the city in ruins and passed by the burned wreckage of the walls and city gates? I wonder how many Jews had passed by Jerusalem and done nothing? I wonder how many hung their heads in shame, but refused to be moved to action? They chose to be ordinary and normal, and to ignore the promptings of their own consciences.

A few years ago, some buddies and I took the second leg of a life-dream to visit every Major League ballpark in America. In

2006, we toured all of the West Coast stadiums, and in 2009 we hit all the East Coast venues. In the summer of 2012, we are hoping to experience seven of the MLB parks around the Great Lakes.

During our East Coast tour, we spent two full days in Washington, D.C., visiting popular tourist sites during the morning and afternoon before games in the evening. On the second morning, the guys in the group wanted to head to Baltimore to catch a tour of Camden Yards, but I stayed in D.C. to meet with a friend from grade school. "Billy" and I had grown up together, but I hadn't seen him in more than ten years, maybe even fifteen. Even though we weren't the same age, Billy had been a great neighbor, and I was sad that we had lost contact.

So I got up early on Saturday morning to walk a few blocks to a metro tunnel. There I would catch a train that would drop me off near the Smithsonian, where Billy and I would meet. I was famished and a few minutes ahead of the train schedule, so I stopped and grabbed a breakfast sub from Subway. As they wrapped up that twelve-inch bundle of goodness, I couldn't wait to sink my teeth into ham, eggs, sizzling bacon and whatever other delicacies they placed on it.

I left the restaurant and resumed my stroll to the underground metro station, taking the first bite of an awesome morning meal. As I prepared for my second bite, I caught a glimpse of something I hadn't seen even once in my full-day tour of D.C. on Friday. Across the street, sitting on the sidewalk in the middle of a very long block, was a lone homeless man. D.C. is a pretty clean city, and street peddlers are "encouraged" to peddle elsewhere. I looked away from him and was immediately struck by a clear message from God: I knew I needed to share my sandwich with that man.

I'm ashamed to say I actually debated whether or not to follow God's lead, but I'm glad to report that God won out over my stomach. I altered my course, crossed the street and then doubled back to where the homeless man was. As I approached, he was a little apprehensive, probably wondering if I was some legal authority about to remove him from the street.

Instead, I opened up the rest of my breakfast sub and asked him if he wanted a bite to eat. He glanced from me to the sandwich a couple of times and then asked me what was on it. He told me he was vegetarian, but when I explained there was only ham and bacon for meats, he assured me "they didn't count as meats," and he politely accepted. I tore the sandwich in half, talked with him for a few minutes while we ate our breakfast together, and then I went on my way.

As I think back to that moment, I'm amazed at how simple that act was, yet how good it made me feel. That man must have thanked me a hundred times before I left his company, and, several times throughout the day, I just smiled when I thought about it. It wasn't that what I did was hard. Sure, I parted with half my breakfast, but truth was — he needed it more than I did. I probably should have offered him the whole thing, yet in the moment that God moved me to act, I responded to God's work in my life through my conscience. The payoff was big for both of us — I was filled with joy, and he was filled with food. That's a real win-win. And, it's the type of thing that happens almost every time we respond with action to the movement of God in our lives.

How's Your Sensitivity?

If you want to live the extraordinary life, you will have to learn to be moved by God by being sensitive to His Word, His Spirit and to the conscience He has placed inside of you. Being normal and ordinary will require none of that, and it will produce in your life the normal results you've always seen. Nehemiah didn't settle for normal, and neither should you!

Summary

Sensitivity to God's Word?

1. Do you have a steady diet of God's Word in your life? If not, here are a few ideas to help you implement a plan for reading and applying the Word:

    - **Schedule it**: Reading God's Word rarely "just happens." Just like every other good discipline in your life, you need to schedule time to be in the book.
    - **Organize it**: Pick a Bible reading plan that works for you. If you're not used to reading the Word regularly, you probably shouldn't start with the Bible in 90 Days program, where you have to read 45-60 minutes every day. You could use a resource like www.tenthdotministries.com (I do some of the writing for this ministry), an online resource to help you connect with God and His Word. You could read a chapter a day in the New Testament and get through all twenty seven books in less than a year. Whatever it is, find a plan that works for you, and can flex with your personal growth and schedule.
    - **Journal it**: Record your thoughts. Write down what you're learning about God, His Word, His Spirit and what He wants you to do. As you learn and grow from reading the Bible, be sure to write it down so you can see it again later. I've often drawn encouragement and hope from rereading my past journal entries. Sometimes I forget what I've learned or how I've grown and journaling allows me to see progress.

2. Do you share your spiritual journey with someone? All of us need accountability so that,as we learn and grow, we also act. I'm thankful for my friend Danny, my wife Traci, my friend and pastor Tim and others who have helped me grow by keeping me accountable for things

I've learned. Make sure you connect with someone who will help you grow.

Sensitivity to God's Spirit?

1. Do you seek the Spirit's leading in your life? In Romans 8, Paul explains that the Spirit prays for us when we don't even know what to pray for (Romans 8:26-27). In 1 Corinthians 2, Paul tells us the Spirit helps us understand the Word of God (1 Corinthians 2:10-15). We must regularly ask for the Spirit's help in our spiritual growth and development.

2. Do you know what the Spirit's leading feels like? Have you heard that "still small voice of God" in your life? In your journal, make sure you record those times you responded to God's leading through His Spirit. I know I have journal entries where I responded to God's leading, and I was thankful; I've also recorded times I ignored the Spirit, and I was filled with regret. Both types of entries remind me to listen to God's Spirit.

Sensitivity to Your Conscience?

1. According to Psalm 139, God created you inside and out, which means He also gave you a conscience. Do you heed your conscience when it tells you to do or not do something? The mind can be a tricky thing, of course, and we should never respond to our inner urgings when they are in violation of God's Word, but God uses that to guide us, too. When was the last time you responded to your conscience?

2. The more we learn to trust in God's Word and God's Spirit, the more refined our conscience will be. Only God can soften or heal a hardened conscience. If yours needs help, spending more time with Him is the place to start.

"God's cause is committed to men; God commits Himself to men. Praying men are the vice-regents of God; they do His work and carry out His plans."
E.M. Bounds

Chapter Three
Powerful Prayers

Nehemiah was moved by God to act. When his brother reported the condition of Jerusalem, Nehemiah was broken and ready to do what it took to see that God's name was honored among the gentiles. I believe anyone could have stepped up and led the charge to see the walls rebuilt, but it was Nehemiah who responded to God's leading. The first principle of *Project Nehemiah* is to allow yourself to be moved by God.

Almost immediately after being moved by God to act, Nehemiah gives us the second principle for those who want to do the extraordinary for God — he began to pray powerful prayers.

Powerful Prayers

Most Christians pray. Whether it's heartfelt communication with the Almighty Creator of the universe or rote memorization, almost all of us pray. But powerful prayers are those prayers that start in our hearts (because we've been moved by God) and flow through our communion with God. It's those prayers that overwhelm us, that break us, that ultimately bring us closer to God. I've watched a dad pray half-heartedly over a meal he was about to eat on one occasion, then pray with tears over the health of his baby girl while sitting in a hospital room awaiting news from a doctor. One prayer was rote. One was powerful.

Powerful Prayers are Passionate

Powerful prayers have a few key characteristics. First, they are steeped in passion, flowing from our desires to see God do something miraculous — something extraordinary! Nehemiah's prayer was passionate. When his heart had been broken by the terrible news of the condition of Jerusalem, he wept, he mourned and he fasted. It was from this heartache that his prayer was birthed: *"When I heard these things, I sat down and wept. For some days I mourned and fasted and prayed before the God of heaven"* (1:4).

Scripture is full of men and women who prayed passionate prayers when moved by God. Paul prayed with joy over the Philippian believers' faith (Philippians 1:4), and he was moved to pray often for his churches (Colossians 1:9). Daniel had friends he urged to *"plead with God"* about the interpretation of a dream (Daniel 2:18), and he himself often begged God for help in his prayers (Daniel 9:3). Hannah wept as she cried out to God *"in bitterness of soul,"* hoping for a child of her own (1 Samuel 1:10). Epaphras *"wrestled"* in prayer for the saints (Colossians 4:12). Jesus was mocked for his passionate prayer life (Psalm 69:9-12), told parables about powerful, passionate prayer (Luke 18:9-14), and He Himself prayed passionately throughout His entire earthly ministry (Luke 22:44). Powerful prayers are passionate.

Powerful Prayers are All About God

In the parable of two prayers told in Luke 18:9-14, Jesus says, *"Two men went up to the temple to pray...the Pharisee stood up and prayed about [to] himself..."* This man looked to heaven. This man knew all the right lingo and sounded somewhat spiritual. By all outward appearances, this was a guy who knew how to pray. This man prayed to himself, for himself, about himself. His prayer meant nothing.

By contrast, the other man *"stood at a distance. He would not even look up to heaven, but beat his breast and said, 'God, have mercy on me, a sinner.'"* This other man didn't look to heaven. This other man probably didn't even know the right prayer lingo, and, honestly, he didn't sound too spiritual. He didn't look like he even knew *how* to pray. This man prayed to God, for God's help, making it all about God. And his prayer was received.

In Numbers 14, the children of Israel rebel against God, and God prepares to bring the lumber. He says to Moses:

> *"How long will these people treat me with contempt?…I will strike them down with a plague and destroy them, but I will make you into a nation greater and stronger than they."*

Moses responds in passionate prayer:

> *"Then the Egyptians will hear about it! By your power you brought these people up from among them…[but] if you put these people to death all at one time, the nations who have heard this report about you will say, 'The Lord was not able to bring these people into the land He promised them on oath…' Now may the Lord's strength be displayed…"* (Numbers 14:11-17)

I've often wondered if Moses ever regretted that prayer before God — he could have had his own nation! But his prayer gives us a vivid reminder of the types of prayer God seeks from His children when He has moved in their hearts. He wants passionate prayers that are all about Him, not about us. Moses declares God's greatness, not his own. Moses elevates God, not himself. Powerful prayers are passionate, and powerful prayers are centered on the nature and character of God.

Look at how Nehemiah elevated God in his prayer:

- God is an awesome God *(1:5).*
- God keeps His covenant of love (1:5).
- God is a forgiving God (1:6).
- God is a promise-keeping God (1:9).
- God is a redeeming God (1:10).

- God is a listening God (1:11).
- God is a powerful God, able to move in the hearts of earthly kings (1:11).

Powerful Prayers Employ God's Power

Like Moses in Numbers 14, like the tax collector in Luke 18, Nehemiah's prayer in Chapter 1 relies entirely on the power of God to act. Nehemiah needed God to forgive his sins and the sins of Israel (1:6-7). Nehemiah needed God to listen to His request (1:6, 11). And ultimately, Nehemiah needed God to grant him success as he laid his plans and dreams before the godless king of Babylon: *"Give your servant success today by granting him favor in the presence of this man"* (1:11).

Later in the story, Nehemiah prays for God to punish those who opposed their project (4:4-5), and he repeatedly prayed for God to provide strength when there seemed to be none (6:9). Nehemiah prayed powerful prayers that could only be answered by the power of God. When that wall was finished, Nehemiah could in no way take the credit — it had to be a God thing!

Powerful Prayers are Persistent

Nehemiah prayed often. It wasn't enough to bring this request one time to God and leave it there; he perpetually beat on the throne room door and pleaded for God's help:

- Nehemiah 1:5-11: Nehemiah seeks forgiveness, God's power and God's glory.
- Nehemiah 2:4: Moments before speaking to the king, Nehemiah asks for God's help to know what to say.
- Nehemiah 4:4-5: Nehemiah asks God to silence the opposition to the building project.
- Nehemiah 6:9: As the project nears completion, Nehemiah requests God's strength to finish the task.
- Nehemiah 6:14: Nehemiah leaves revenge in God's hands, trusting His jurisdiction over the enemies of Israel.

The writer of Hebrews says, "*Let us then approach the throne of grace with confidence, so that we may receive mercy and find grace to help us in our time of need*" (Hebrews 4:16). The death of Jesus Christ opened the curtain that protected the throne room of grace. When Jesus died, the curtain was torn in two, and He created access for all of God's children to go directly to the Father to seek grace and mercy in times of need.

Jesus Himself had a little something to say about persistent prayers. In Luke 18, He told the story of a woman seeking justice. In fact, Luke introduces this parable by saying: "*Then Jesus told His disciples a parable to show them that they should always pray and not give up*" (Luke 18:1). In the story, a widow seeks justice, day and night, from a judge who doesn't particularly care about or fear God. But her persistence wears him down, and finally he grants her justice so she'll leave him alone.

The point is clear: if the ungodly judge will grant justice out of convenience, how much more will the God of the universe, the Holy and Just Creator, respond to His children? The throne room of grace is open! God wants you to come freely, boldly and repeatedly, seeking His help.

The Source of Powerful Prayers

If you have already put your faith in Jesus' death, burial and resurrection as sufficient payment for your sins, this access is already yours. You don't have to go to your pastor or priest to gain access to God; you can speak to the Father now — anytime! — because of the blood of Jesus Christ.

If you haven't put your faith in Jesus' sacrifice for you, if you haven't had access to God's throne room of grace, you could change all of that in a moment. Simply come to God on His terms and admit that you have violated His law — you have lived an imperfect life, but God can enter into this life-changing relationship with you only if you have been perfect (Romans 3:23). One imperfection (the Bible calls this sin) is enough to keep you and God separated forever.

This sin problem is complicated by the fact that you can't personally change anything about it. Because you are imperfect, you can't mediate different terms. Not only are you separated from God now, but you will continue to be separated. Even if you wanted to enter the throne room and connect with God, the door would remain closed to you.

God knew this was the case for you and me and all other human beings in history. So He sent His Son Jesus to remedy our sin problem (John 3:16). Jesus did what you and I couldn't do — He lived a perfect life so He could be the perfect sacrifice. When He died on the cross, He was a perfect man paying the price, not for *His* sins, but for *our* sins. He died so we wouldn't have to. Three days later, He rose again and, in doing so, he gave access to God for any who would put their faith and trust in Him.

Today you can begin a new life with God. Tell Him you are imperfect, that you have broken His law. Admit to Him that there is nothing you can do to change your present condition and that you don't want to spend eternity separated from Him. Then thank Him for sending Jesus to bridge the gap, making salvation possible. Believe in faith that Jesus rose from the dead, conquering sin and death and opening God's home to you (Romans 10:9-10). Left to yourself, you are doomed; through Jesus, you have access. Receive this great gift today!

Powerful Prayers Illustrated

After I graduated from high school in 1992, I made plans to attend a Christian liberal arts university, where I intended to pick up a degree in medicine, as well as a degree in youth ministry. *My plan* was simple. I was already confident God had called me into youth ministry, and I had decided that I wanted to do youth ministry in towns and communities where they couldn't afford to hire a full-time youth pastor. By getting a degree in medicine, I knew I could work practically anywhere and make a decent salary to support my family, while doing youth ministry on the side. The plan was good.

It just wasn't God's plan.

Midway through the summer of 1992, I developed one of the only significant illnesses I remember having: I contracted mono. Or more correctly, mono got me. I was totally laid up for three full weeks. I remember sleeping 16-20 hours a day as my body shut down general operations in an attempt to repair itself. Once my oldest brother Dan came by the house and dropped off some pizza for me. When I refused pizza, his face froze — he knew something was dreadfully wrong. I believe that was the first and last time I've ever refused free pizza.

Between bouts of sweet slumber, a question began popping into my head again and again. I kept asking myself this: I have good plans for my life…but are they *God's plans* for my life? It was the first time I had ever stopped to wonder if what I was doing was truly from God, or if it was just my bright idea. It wasn't that choosing to be a youth pastor with a secondary vocation was inherently a bad idea; I just started wondering if my plan was inherently *God's* plan. By the end of my championship bout with mono, I had spent some quality time with God and was certain of this: *My plans* were good, but His were better, and they didn't include a degree in medicine.

Instead of the large Christian university I chose in Ohio, God sent me to a relatively small Bible school in a corn field in Iowa. My triumphant victory over mono came somewhere around the mid-point of August, so when I called Faith Baptist Bible College and asked about admissions, they were a little surprised and hesitant since school started in less than a week. I prayed and spent time talking to my parents. Finally, we all agreed that going to college in Iowa was God's plan, and I began packing for school.

I called Faith again and told them I had filled out the application, and, instead of mailing it, I would simply bring it with me since it would take the same amount of time to get there whether the U.S. Postal Service carried it or I brought it in person. Because my friends Craig and Jason were already enrolled in the school, I let the school know I would travel with those two. The dean informed me that I was welcome to come to the school, but I needed to know that if my application was turned down, I would not be allowed to stay on campus. I didn't have the heart to tell him, but I knew God had already approved my application. I was going to school!

Faith Baptist Bible College proved to be the perfect place for me. It was a tough, conservative school, and God used it to smooth out some of my rough edges. I had to learn to abide by a code of conduct that wasn't one I would necessarily adopt personally or professionally, but one I had to agree with in order to be a student. Some of the classes were challenging, and several professors pushed me hard, including the head of all youth ministries majors, Pastor Don Bartemus. It was through his help and guidance that I was able to juggle my schedule and finish four years' worth of schooling in only three years. I was eager to get into youth ministry.

After graduation, I ran into a problem I hadn't anticipated: churches weren't particularly eager to hire young, single youth pastors. After several closed doors, God opened one at a camp back home in the Pacific Northwest. Camp Glendawn had a new director, and they were seeking a program director to work through the summer of 1995. I wasn't thrilled with the idea at first — I wanted to be a youth pastor — but, once again, God made it clear that His path was different from mine.

Saddled with quite a bit of personal debt and student loans, I left Iowa, returned to the Northwest and jumped into my new job as the program director of a summer camp. It was truly a life-changing experience and an awesome first summer of ministry. I fell in love with camping ministry, and, as the Seattle Mariners were making a historic run at the playoffs at summer's end in 1995, I was already preparing for the summer of 1996.

The fall of 1995, however, proved more challenging than I had anticipated. Camping life slows to a crawl in the fall, with groups coming in only on weekends. I spent my Friday nights doing group orientation, and my Saturdays were spent helping the director and his wife wash dishes and set up for meals in the kitchen. John and JoAnn and their two daughters became great friends, and my life and ministry were shaped by their love and support during the year we served together.

As we moved from fall to winter that year, the camp entered some serious financial difficulties. In fact, for several months they were unable to make payroll. Once again God stepped in and showed that His plan was still best. School loans were coming due, along with some credit card debt I had accumulated while trying to stay in school, and I had no means to pay those bills without income. John and JoAnn came to the rescue again, when John took any extra income that came in to ensure that I got paid. In fact, although he would probably deny it, I'm sure he took money from his own personal resources to make sure I was paid, so I could make my debt payments. Clearly this wasn't *my plan* of action, but God was proving that His plan was better because *He* could make it work!

In January 1996, I began having some of the sweetest moments with God that I had ever had. Each morning as I would start with His Word and an extended time of prayer, I began asking for the impossible. I asked God to somehow, some way, pay off half of my student loans. I shared this request with no one but God. I prayed it daily and relentlessly for months, believing that if God had truly changed my plans for college, if God had clearly directed me to a Bible camp instead of a local church youth group, if God knew He was placing me in what appeared to be a dire financial circumstance — then I believed He could settle half my loans in a heartbeat. So I prayed faithfully.

In late spring 1996, God's plan seemed to develop a wrinkle. As the camp was still struggling under financial pressures and lack of strong leadership from the board, a decision was reached to sell the property and closeup shop. God provided a buyer from Southern California who paid the full asking price and, included a provision in the purchase, that a gift should be made for our local Northwest Bible seminary. By mid-April, I was out of work and back in my parents' house in Salem, Oregon, where I continued to pray for God to pay half of my student loan.

About a month after the camp sold, the former chairman of the board called me, somewhat out of the blue. We chatted for a few minutes, and he asked me about my work and where I was headed next before he told me he had good news. When the camp had been sold, after the mortgage had been paid off and money had been donated to the seminary and another local Christian camp, a few bucks remained in the checking account. The board had met and, in a unanimous decision, they had decided to give me an extra gift: they wanted to pay half of my student loans.

My jaw dropped to the floor. I was stunned. I thanked him for the call and hung up. I was shocked.

And angry.

I was shocked because I had shared my six-month prayer request with no one. God was the only one who knew of my impossible request. The fact that these men came together and chose "half" as their desired gift was nothing short of a miracle. In an instant, God had revealed His power and His ability to carry out His plan with that power.

But I was also angry. In nothing short of divine clarity, I hung up the phone and realized how faithless I had been. To this day, I am confident that God let me pray that prayer for six months, not because He was slow in working out His plan, but because He was giving me 180 days to ask for the *whole* amount! I later learned that enough money had remained, after the sale of the camp and the distribution of gifts to the seminary and the other camp, to pay my entire student debt five times over — and I had the gall to ask...for half? God didn't pay half because *His resources* were limited; He paid half because *my faith* was limited! To this day I have never forgotten the moment when I sat in my parents' kitchen with the reality sinking in that God could do more than I could ever imagine or guess or request in my wildest dreams. To this day my wife and I have a saying as we live out our overboard lives before God: don't pray for half!

That illustration reminds me of the mercy and grace God extends to those who pray powerful prayers, and it validates the principles seen in God's Word. I prayed with passion for God to impact that financial situation. During those days in cabin #7, I made my prayers about God and His greatness, not me and my debt. I employed God to do what only He could do, provide in ways I couldn't imagine or foresee. And believe me, I prayed persistently. Every day I had taken that request to God.

Your Prayer Life

What is your prayer life like? Are you praying powerful prayers as they pertain to the movement of God in your heart and to the dreams He has given you? Take some time to evaluate your prayer life according to the pattern of powerful prayers in God's Word.

Passionate

1. When was the last time you were moved to pray? What were the circumstances that led to that prayer?

2. The more we grow in our walk with God, the more we are moved by the things that move Him. If you want to grow in your passionate prayers, stay close to God!

God-focused

1. Are your prayers God-focused or you-focused? One way to get a good gauge of that is to write out some prayers to God. I'm amazed at how often I do that and see the words "I" or "me" or "my" or "mine" pop up in the written prayers. Look at Nehemiah's prayer in

Nehemiah 1:5-11. Nehemiah makes just five references to himself. Two come in the context of confession of sin, three in the context of his main request — *"God give me success before the king."* By contrast, over twenty times he makes reference to God! Write out your prayers and evaluate them: are they God-focused?

2. Another way to develop God-focused prayers is to pray according to Jesus' pattern set in the Lord's Prayer of Matthew 6. I like to use the vowels as a reminder:

    - A = Admit your sin to God. Begin your prayer by confessing your failures to God.
    - E = Exalt God. Praise God for who He is. Worship Him for His greatness.
    - I = Implore God. Ask God for help, for mercy, for grace, for power.
    - O = Offer thanksgiving to God. Thank Him in advance for hearing and answering your prayers.
    - U = Utilize the Spirit. Ask the Spirit for help in your prayers.

God's Power

1. When you pray, are you seeking God's power in your life or just hoping your good qualities will manage to shine through? I love Nehemiah's prayer in 6:9: *"But I prayed, 'Now strengthen my hands.'"* He was praying for God to be the source of his strength. He wasn't praying that his own strength would be enough; he knew he didn't have enough strength. Instead, he prayed for God's strength to be enough. Are you praying for your power to be on display, or for God's?

2. As you think about asking God to show His power, do this little exercise. Imagine that God answers your prayer(s) exactly as you have prayed them. Write out the answers to these two questions. First, how will God's power be shown through this request? Second, how will

you praise God in order to make sure the glory is His and not yours? If we learn to anticipate God's answer to our prayers by thinking through how His name would be praised, I am confident we will learn to make our prayers more about His power and less about ours.

Persistent Prayer

1. The ungodly judge granted a request simply because the widow was persistent. God is a just God, and He responds to His children out of mercy and grace. Are you regularly taking your request(s) to God? Don't allow His silence or perceived lack of action to be an excuse to stop praying. Seek God early and often as you pray powerful prayers. Right now, schedule some time to take these requests to God. For one prayer request I took before God, I scheduled myself to pray at the top of each hour. At 7 a.m. I prayed; at 8 a.m., I prayed; at 9, 10, 11, noon, 1 p.m., etc., I prayed. Those were short prayers, but they were passionate and persistent.

2. Jesus' gracious sacrifice makes access to the throne room possible. Don't be a stranger to God's presence! How often do you pray? Like any habit, prayer is hard work. I encourage my students to learn how to pray by doing this: I tell them to set a timer for five minutes. (For some, we start with three minutes!) Then I tell them to pray until the timer goes off, and, when it goes off, to say "Amen" and to stop praying. I encourage them to do this twice a day. After 7-10 days, I encourage them to add one minute to their prayer time, moving it to six minutes a session, twice a day. Again, they do this for 7-10 days, and then they add more time. Over the period of thirty days, a student's prayer life will go from 1-2 minutes a day, to 18-20 minutes a day (in two 9-10 minute prayer sessions). Over a period of six months, students will be praying upwards of thirty minutes a day. Often I hear them say, "I couldn't believe thirty minutes was over

when the timer went off!" Persistent prayer takes discipline, and you can begin that in five minute blocks.

"We grow by dreams. All big men are dreamers."
Woodrow T. Wilson

Chapter Four
Ginormous Dreams

The first principle we learn from Nehemiah is that we must allow ourselves to be moved by God, and once moved, we must act. It's not enough to *feel* sympathy or empathy if it doesn't result in action. Sometimes it's an action we weren't expecting to take; other times it's part of our very DNA. Great things get done for God when His people are moved to act by the things that move God.

The second principle is that once moved to act, we must surround our emotions and actions with powerful prayer. Prayer aligns our hearts with God, so we can check our motives and pride at the door. Powerful prayer reminds us to act for God's glory, not ours, and powerful prayer results in others rising up to join us. Many well-meaning Christians and good people are stirred in their hearts to act, but fail to fall on their knees in prayer. Modern-day Nehemiahs do both.

The third principle is to start dreaming ginormous, God-sized dreams. I have seen this principle played out in the lives of God's children over and over again. Sometimes I see it played out through my pastoral ministry; other times I've read about it in the works and lives of those who have gone before us. This third principle is often the place where miracles are birthed.

CT's Dreams

I enjoy reading. I try to add a little method to my madness when I read so I don't read only one genre. A few years ago I added life stories to the list of genres I liked, and I started engaging in the biographies of great men and women of the faith. One year, after finishing a book about pastoral theology, I decided to tackle a biography. I found one I knew nothing about sitting on my shelf. I had picked up the book from a sweet widow in Iowa, who had asked me to take some of her husband's ministry books shortly after he passed away. He had been in ministry for many years, and she wanted his books to be given to those in ministry or to those preparing for ministry as I was. The book had been on my shelf for years, but I had never read it.

The book was called *C.T. Studd* and was written by Norman Grubb. I had never heard of C.T. Studd, but when I saw he was once a great cricketer (one who plays cricket, not one who hunts crickets!), I was intrigued; my love of sport got me hooked. Grubb's description of Studd and his life was fascinating, convicting and at times troubling.

C.T. Studd was indeed an excellent cricket player who had the potential to have a professional career in the sport. However, when the Lord got a hold of his life while he was still in school, Studd offered his entire being to the service of the Lord and immediately began preparing for life as a missionary. Soon after salvation, C.T. was headed to China to do mission work, and he spent much of the next twenty years of his life serving God in China. His love for missions grew.

After leaving China, he returned home to England, married a fine woman, was soon blessed with his first daughter and began preparing for something else: another mission work. But this time, it would be in a land that was relatively unreached with the Gospel. C.T. became one of the great trailblazers in the land of Africa, in the region of Chad. The impact of his turn-of-the-century ministry is still felt today, over 100 years after he began to serve God.

C.T. and his wife had big dreams for Africa. He was confident of God's call in his life, and confident that God had carefully orchestrated the events of his life to prepare him for this next stage. With full assurance of spirit and passion, C.T. began speaking throughout all of England, raising up an army of student missionaries and trying to fund the next phase of his journey. His desire was to start a new mission whose goal was to reach Africa with the Gospel. He didn't just want to blaze a trail to walk on; he wanted to blaze a trail an entire army could march through! He regularly pleaded with God to save Africa.

At one point, C.T. had purchased his passage by boat and rail to India, where he would then take passage to Africa. However, before he could secure the permits, resources and team members necessary to see the success of this venture to Chad, he needed another 10,000 pounds (Today, 10,000 pounds is roughly equivalent to $15,550). His dreams were big, his obstacles seemed even bigger, but he knew His God was biggest!

The night before he was to depart, C.T. and his wife prayed for God's provision, as he was still in need of 10,000 pounds. That night, C.T. had a dream in which God assured him the money would arrive. C.T. needed to simply go to the train station and leave England in faith. God promised to provide. C.T. woke, had breakfast with his wife, and they shared in one last time of prayer together.

Shortly after their sweet closing moments, the cabbie arrived to take C.T. to the train station. He sat on a bench and awaited his train, confident that God's power would be shown. Soon his train pulled into the station. C.T. gathered his meager belongings and prepared to board. As he did, he noticed another horse and buggy moving rapidly to the station. He watched as a man excitedly jumped off and called out, "Has anyone seen a Mr. C.T. Studd?"

C.T. Studd smiled.

The man on the buggy came toward C.T. and offered him a large suitcase, with 10,000 pounds inside. C.T. had never met the man. And prior to the previous night, the man had never heard of C.T. While C.T. had been having a dream in which God promised to provide for his ministry needs, this man was being tormented by his own dream, one in which God told him plainly that he was to take 10,000 pounds to the train station the next morning and give it to a man he had never met. Each time the gentleman woke, he told God "no way," but when he fell asleep, he returned to the same dream. Finally, in the middle of the night, he surrendered to God, and promised to take the money to the train station first thing in the morning and give it to a stranger named C.T. Studd.

As the man explained his story, C.T.'s dreams for Africa started to become reality. You see, God had carefully prepared Studd for big things in Africa. His preparation at school through cricket, through Bible Society meetings, and through his ministry in China — all of it was part of God's plan to take him to Africa to blaze new trails. In turn, C.T. understood that God's preparation was so much bigger than he could fathom, and that God's ability to provide would surpass any scheme Studd could put together. So C.T. left the provisions to God and spent his time dreaming about what ministry in Africa might look like.

The third principle we learn from the story of Nehemiah is that we must dream improbable dreams. Too often we put God in a tiny little yard with big electric fences because of what *we think* can or cannot be done. Instead of trusting in His work and His power to accomplish what He has prepared us for, we start looking into the mirror to size up our options. That is not what C.T. did, and definitely not what Nehemiah did. C.T. believed so strongly in his God-given dreams for Africa that he went to the train station and waited for God to show up.

By contrast, I'm afraid that all too often we sit at home. We tell God, "If you will bring the 10,000 pounds to the house, then I'll believe what you're doing and go to Africa." God isn't looking for more of His children to play it safe or to trust in what they can see and handle before they decide to *go*. As we learn to trust Him, He paves a path for us to march on. He carefully guides us through the ups and downs of our experiences, and then He brings us to the edge and tells us to take a leap of faith — not a blind jump, but a jump that requires faith based on the ways we have seen God act in our lives in the past.

Nehemiah's Dreams

Nehemiah didn't play it safe. When his brother told him what happened in Israel, Nehemiah's heart was moved and he began to pray powerful prayers. As you look at those prayers, you'll see Nehemiah's enormous dream unfold:

> *"O Lord, let your ear be attentive to the prayer of this your servant and to the prayer of your servants who delight in revering your name. Give your servant success today by granting him favor in the presence of this man [the king]."* (Nehemiah 1:11)

Upon hearing the news of Israel, Nehemiah fasted and prayed for several days. Then, moments before his next duty to the king, he was already dreaming about making a change. He wasn't waiting for someone else to step up to the plate. He wasn't sitting around wondering who would act first — he knew his path had been marked by God, and it was time for him to lay out his dreams before the One who could accomplish them.

And Nehemiah didn't pray for half. He didn't size up the dream and then cut it down to size. I'm confident many believers pray like that — afraid to tax God with too much "work." Nehemiah's faith was too big to have pint-sized dreams and prayers!

So Nehemiah prays his dream to God: *"Grant me success."* Give me the king's ear. Move in his will to help us. Soften his heart to our cause. And as Nehemiah's conversation with the king unfolds, God starts to work, and Nehemiah's dream begins to take shape. By the time he was done talking with the king, Nehemiah had been given time off from work, building materials to start and finish the project, and promise of safe passage throughout the realm.

Your Dreams

What dreams has God placed in your heart? How has God brought you to where you are right now, at this moment, in order to do what only He can do, just as He did with Nehemiah?

Take time to write out your journey you have been on so far. This isn't necessarily the time or the book to work out the pain from your past (*Project Joseph,* the first book of this Life Improvement Series, is all about dealing with past pain). Instead, it's the time to see how God has taken your whole journey — yes, the good, the bad, the great and the horribly ugly — to bring you to this place, at this time.

As you do this, think about your journey in two parts: first, the facts of your journey — what has *actually* happened to bring you to this place? Here's an example of how I would list some key events from my life:

1. Began a relationship with God while attending a Christian school in kindergarten.
2. Desired to be a youth pastor because of the godly influence of my junior high youth pastor, Bob Smith.
3. Was given leadership opportunities to grow, serve and learn with my high school youth pastor, Kevin Moyer.
4. Enjoyed growing up in a godly home with two parents who loved God.
5. Exposed to pornography at a young age and struggled with this life-entangling sin for years.
6. Experienced significant spiritual growth through three years at Bible school.
7. Developed a deepening trust for God when I ended up working at Bible camp instead of with a youth group.
8. Learned the painful lesson of praying for half, instead of trusting God for all.

9. Became friends with Danny Ray, a gifted dreamer who asked me to join his writing ministry.
10. Wrote my first book, *Project Joseph,* and launched Overboard Ministries.

Once you've written out the list of facts, here is the second step: write out how each of these facts has affected who you are today.

I can look at each one of those ten facts (and the many more that I would write out if I were doing this assignment) and see how God has used each one in my life to bring me to this point, at this time. Some of those facts bring back great memories. Some of them are incredibly painful. A couple of them make me smile and cry at the same moment, depending on which angle I'm seeing. The point is that each of these key moments of your life has shaped you. You are where you are today because of the series of events that have unfolded in your life and how, right or wrong, you have responded to those moments.

Here's the cool part of this exercise: as you do this, you will see patterns emerge in the work God has done in and through you. Maybe those patterns exist primarily because of painful experiences, but out of those you can now see that God wants to use that for something great in your life. When I look at the facts of my life, two big patterns emerge. The first is that God put youth ministry deep in my heart. He planted a passion for working with young people, even while I was still one of those young people! He set my heart aflame for youth ministry, and that fire still burns bright and hot today.

The second pattern I see is that God has put me in key relationships at precise moments in my life to direct me to the next phase of my journey. Bob was instrumental in creating a youth ministry passion in my heart, and P.K. was the one God used to hone and develop it. The list of influencers for me goes well beyond my ten-point list: Glen Chapman challenged me to think about the whys of tradition; Sharon Lewis trusted me with huge responsibilities long before I thought I was ready to handle them (and probably long before I was ready, but that was part of the lesson); my brother Phil made me think logically and doctrinally to be able to answer his questions, and he showed me what humility looked like even when I didn't display it; Kendy taught me about true friendship; Don Bartemus pushed me to test the walls of what is "normal" in ministry; my wife Traci has repeatedly been the right person at the right time to catapult me to the next place by challenging me to not live a mediocre life; Mel gave me a chance to write; Andy won't let me settle for average ministry; and Danny forced me to think outside the box. The list could go on, but I think you get the point.

As I look at the key events of my life, I see how God brought the right people at the right time to shift my thinking, change my perceptions, sharpen my doctrine or humble my arrogance. In this pattern, I recognize that when someone "just comes along" in my life with insights or ideas, I try to pay extra close attention, knowing that God has used people in my life over and over again.

As you look at your list, what patterns do you see, and how do those patterns influence your dreams? The final part of this exercise is to write out your God-designed and God-sized dreams. What are they? What patterns have emerged in your life that show the fingerprint of God as He has brought you to this place, at this time? How has God used even your worst moments to create beauty in your life?

Psalm 139 reminds us that every facet of our lives is significant and planned. God knows it all, and nothing that happens to us occurs apart from His awareness and His planning. God knows everything about our creation, including the details of our physical bodies, our emotional makeup and even the composition of our personalities (Psalm 139:13-15). God knows it all because He created us! Not only does He know us inside and out, He also knows everything about our past and future, including those events and relationships that have or will have a profound impact on who we are. He knows all of our days and hours and minutes (Psalm 139:16); nothing escapes Him.

God's infinite knowledge allows us to trust Him fully. Even our deepest pains become powerful tools in shaping our lives and dreams when they are given over to the Creator. I'm confident that as you complete these exercises, you will see God's hand in shaping you and your heart for His work. Then, as you allow your heart to be moved by Him — because you see how He has shaped you — your dreams will take shape.

Cherrie's Dreams

Cherrie continues to be amazed at how God is using her and her dreams to reach people in Korah. While 24/7 living in Korah doesn't seem to be the door God has opened for her, she has dreams of more expansive work. Some of her work might include development of a medical clinic. One of her jobs is to keep raising awareness here at home and helping people understand the overwhelming need for project teams, medical missions, funds for education and building, and the need for people to simply visit Korah to build relationships with the community.

In fact, Cherrie said that home-visits in Korah mean the world to the people, as others share God's love and offer them theirs. Families and individuals in Korah will remember visits, and visitors, more than a year later!

As Cherrie has had the opportunity to introduce people to Korah, she says that taking them to the dump is an experience that cannot be described with words. The trash dump is the center of the community, and most of the people of Korah live either on or around the giant pile of garbage. In order to grasp the magnitude of its height and breadth, to get to the top of the dump heap, it takes a fit person thirty minutes from the backside. Once there, the stench is nearly overwhelming, and it is not uncommon for first-time visitors from the West to vomit in revulsion. After visitors get their bearings, they look out almost as far as the eye can see, and all they behold is trash: trash on trash with more trash. And as they look more carefully, these travelers see movement among the trash and realize they are witnessing people, many of whom are children, foraging for their daily existence. Getting people to walk to the top of the dump heap is no easy task, but, once they are there, Cherrie no longer has to ask them to help — it's impossible for them *not* to.

As Cherrie has seen God complete the first of many building projects to house orphans, she is dreaming of what's next. She grabs eager servants by the dozens and takes them to the garbage heap, to what the first Young Lifers called "the pit of hell," and lets the stench of death and filth of children finding "nourishment" from trash do the talking. While Cherrie may not be the one to build the next phase of work in Korah (and she joyfully points out that King David didn't get to build the temple, but he prepared it for his son), she might be the one to introduce the next Nehemiah to the project. So she keeps dreaming!

"Facts are stubborn things; and whatever may be our wishes, our inclinations, or the dictates of our passion, they cannot alter the state of facts and evidence."
John Adams

Chapter Five
Honest Assessment

For many of us, dreams are easy. I'm a natural dreamer, so thinking up big, creative ideas isn't hard. My wife and I love to brainstorm and sometimes come up with wacky thoughts, but that's part of the dreaming process. It's amazing how often the craziest ideas soon become the ones we pursue most passionately as we see God's hand at work in the details.

Once you've been moved to action, have begun to pray powerful prayers and have those ginormous dreams laid out in front of you, it's time to take the next step — the step that kills many God-sized dreams and ideas. It's this step where many believers abandon the ideals of living outside the comfort of the boat and settle for living ordinary lives out of fear, doubt, worry or laziness. It's the step where we need to assess the facts of our situation.

Keep in mind, we are just after the facts. This isn't the time to start guessing at what might or might not happen (speculation); it's the time to figure out where we are now in relationship to where we want to be later (facts). Data gathering isn't very glamorous, nor is it always desirable. In fact, I often have to draw on the strengths and passions of others when it comes to this part of my journey. My wife is a great fact-gatherer. She likes data. She likes charts. She likes researching things. Not me. I like pizza. I like loud conversations and big dreams. I like jumping into something and figuring out the facts later. Maybe God knew I'd need someone like Traci — the perfect soul-mate.

Nehemiah gathered facts, and, as he did, he avoided two key pitfalls that can come upon those who love to languish in data, those who take baths in research papers and actually *want* to upload information to Wikipedia. While I make light of my fact-gathering friends, I recognize how crucial data is as we pursue our God-sized dreams. "God is a God of math," my brother often reminds me. Yet many Christians have never made it past this fourth principle because of the following two obstacles: Fact/Meaning and Getting Bogged Down.

Fact/Meaning

The first obstacle you must overcome when you start your honest assessment comes when you identify each specific fact of your situation. In most cases, it's not gathering the facts that presents the obstacle — it's how we process the facts that can make them obstacles, as we try to pursue the dreams God has given us.

For example, a few years back my wife and I were invited to South Africa to minister at a Bible camp, do some youth worker training and share in the work our friends were doing with orphans and AIDS patients. We decided to take our three kids for what was truly a life-changing trip, and my mom came along as well; her training as a nurse and her ability as an awesome cook and incredible hostess would prove invaluable throughout our 19 day adventure.

After the initial invitation by our friends, convinced of God's leading, we started praying powerful prayers. Through that process, we developed a big dream to take our whole family on this journey to South Africa. The time came when we needed to assess the facts. The first fact was easy: we needed to know how much it would cost to get there. I called my favorite local travel agent, a woman who knows the business inside and out and saves me hours of Internet research. I asked Kim how much flights would cost. Gulp...$2,000 a ticket. That meant we were going to need to raise over $10,000 just for our family to get to South Africa. That wouldn't include any money we wanted to give to the missionaries, so we didn't impact *their* budgets. That wouldn't include any spending money. That wouldn't include any money for a game park visit (which was a must!); that would just put us on the ground in Durban. Yikes! We could never raise that much money in eight months! Maybe Traci and I would have to leave the kids behind. Maybe we would take our oldest son, but leave the two girls with their cousins. Maybe...

Whoops! I just did it. You see, I went from the facts to the meaning of the facts in one breath. In one moment I'm asking Kim for the price of a ticket (fact); in the next moment I'm assigning all sorts of truths (meaning) to those facts. When we assess the facts, we are simply gathering data about the reality of the current situation. We don't need to assign any value to those facts; we just need to know what they are. We also don't need to sugar-coat the facts. The facts are quite simply... just the facts.

Traci and I did more research, and eventually Kim was able to get us tickets at around $1,750 for the adults, and a little under $1,300 for the kids. The actual cost to fly to South Africa was around $8,000 when all taxes and fees were applied. Still, $8,000 *just to get there* was a lot of money. We also knew from others who had gone that we'd need around $1,000 to cover our basic expenses and another $1,000 for spending money, game park entrance fees, fuel, etc. So we were back at needing around $10,000.

The next fact was another easy one: we didn't have $10,000, so we were going to need to raise it (another fact). We looked at a lot of options. We knew our awesome church would support us with gifts and an offering, but we also didn't want to tax the church people for the bulk of this trip. We started a Facebook page, and people both inside and outside the church jumped on board for our regular updates. The word was spreading, and people were getting excited for us to go. It was cool to see how God was working out the details.

Then one afternoon, while sifting through junk mail, I had an idea that we should hold a fun run to help generate income. Time to assess the facts again.

1. We had never hosted a fun run in our lives.
2. Traci had run in a couple, but I had no clue what was involved.
3. Salem already had more than 50 runs each year. How would ours get attention?
4. Runs cost money to put on: park rental fees, insurance fees, city permits, etc.

Those were the facts. But it was also a fact that God was behind the dream to get to South Africa, so we quit assigning our own meanings and started pressing on with God's help.

We came up with a creative run concept in our city's largest and most beautiful park. We designed a unique course, changed the length of the race from a typical 5k or 10k to a 6.21k, and ran the race on June 21 (6/21). We even started the race at 6:21p.m. — a 6.21k on 6/21 at 6:21. People in the racing community thought it was unusual, and we had an unbelievable turnout for a first-year event. One racer told us, "I run 50-60 events a year, including 8-10 new races each year. I have never been a part of a first-year event that was so creative, so fun and so well-organized." We raised over $3,500 in one night. If we had assigned our own meanings to the facts of the race, we might never have seen God work out the details so powerfully.

Moment by moment, in preparation for Africa, God provided gifts, fundraising ideas, special offerings, speaking engagement honorariums and unmarked envelopes left in my box at work, each moving us closer and closer to covering the expenses of our trip. One week after we returned from our trip, the last few dollars came in from our church, and the entire trip had been paid for. God took care of the details; we just needed to get the facts.

Believe me, Traci and I sometimes wondered whether or not taking the whole family was wise. On more than one occasion, even as late as September (just two months before departure), we wondered if taking the kids was going to work financially. At that point, we had raised only about $6,500 and were running out of ideas to raise the extra $3,500 we would need. Again, our struggle was that we were assigning value and meaning to the facts instead of trusting God to take care of those details.

God had moved in our hearts. We were praying powerful prayers. God's work was producing huge dreams. The point of assessing the truth was not to let the facts change the reality of the work God has already done; it was to understand the magnitude of the need for God's mighty hand of grace. For Traci and me, $10,000 was an almost insurmountable goal in such a short time. The facts reminded us that we needed God to turn this into a life-changing experience.

Nehemiah took a similar approach when assessing the facts at the end of Chapter 2. Notice what is recorded in verses 13-18:

> *"By night I went out through the Valley Gate…examining the walls of Jerusalem, which had been broken down, and its gates, which had been destroyed by fire."*
>
> *"Then I moved on toward the Fountain Gate…but there was not enough room for my mount to get through."*
>
> *"Finally, I turned back and reentered through the Valley Gate."*

Notice that in each instance, only the facts are recorded. Maybe Nehemiah felt defeated when he saw the real condition of things, but, based on the next passage, I doubt it. During his nighttime mission, he simply assessed the reality of the current situation: "Walls broken down, gates destroyed by fire, debris so bad you can't get a horse through." No meaning; just facts.

Stepping out in faith and trusting God to work things out doesn't mean we should check our brains at the door. For some Christians, faith and intellectual reason are two mutually exclusive ideas, when in fact, they are two sides of the same coin. When Nehemiah stepped out in faith to rebuild the walls of Jerusalem and to set its gates in place, he didn't just show up and start building without some kind of plan. He took time to honestly assess the facts, so that even though he was clearly stepping out in faith, he was doing so using the mind and talents God had given him.

Assigning our own meaning to the facts is the first pitfall we must avoid when gathering data.

Bogging Down

The second obstacle we must avoid is that of getting bogged down in the facts. I know some of you reading this are processors: you like to analyze data, create charts, make spreadsheets, build infrastructure and clean your desk each night (sickos!) before bed. When you read the first part of this chapter, you salivate — assessing facts and collecting data are your specialty. It's how God wired you.

The second key problem with fact-gathering is that it can also bring progress to a screeching halt. It's possible to spend so much time gathering facts, assessing inventory and exploring opportunities that we never get the actual event/activity/project underway. We get bogged down in data. We put too much emphasis on what we *can* see and not enough on the One we *cannot* see.

I remember being in a board meeting at our church where we were discussing how to add on to our building. We had spent a couple of meetings gathering data, getting bids from contractors, and we had assigned a young man in the church to put together a presentation with all the facts. After several weeks (months?), we all met to see his presentation. In 30 minutes, he showed us sketches that fit within our budget (we were trying to pay cash), pictures of similar projects done by the same company at other churches, and details about how the addition would attach to our present facility. He also included a few extra expenses, which would require some creative fundraising.

He did a great job and had accomplished all that we had asked him to do. But I'll never forget how discouraged I was when questions and comments started coming in. It wasn't that it was a bad idea to double-check the math or verify the proposal, but in that meeting we got so bogged down with the details and with assessing data that we put a halt to the project for another two months. We sent this young man and his team back to reassess the facts and data they had already meticulously gathered. At the end of the eight weeks, we were right back where we had been at his first presentation, and we voted to move forward on the exact same project he had presented to us before!

Now some would argue that we needed to *be sure* of our research, but I would argue that we *were*. This man and his team had done tedious work to gather information. They had met with the builders and contractors; they had toured other facilities. The facts were well-established; it was time to accept or reject the proposal, not time to gather more facts. Again, gathering facts is crucial because we don't want to be reckless or wasteful in our work for the Lord. But fact-gathering should not stop the progress or work of faith. Facts and faith must work hand in hand.

I think back to Cherrie's story and realize how easy it would have been for her to get bogged down with the facts. After visiting Ethiopia for the first time and getting to spend an extra two weeks of bonus vacation in the dump of Korah, she could have walked away overwhelmed by the facts. Almost 130,000 people call Korah home (fact). Thousands of people forage in the dump each day (fact). One boy's dream to house a few dozen scavengers doesn't begin to touch the problem (fact). Leprosy and TB are difficult to combat without expensive medications and extensive follow-up care (fact). On and on, the facts revealed that one person couldn't put a dent in the problems of Korah; the simple facts could have bogged her down to a life of inactivity.

But they didn't. The facts reminded her of the magnitude of God's grace that would be required for any work to have a lasting impact on the children and adults of Korah. The facts refined her dream and strengthened her resolve. The facts acted as a compass for her faith, giving her a direction to begin to act, while allowing God to handle the details.

In Nehemiah's case, look at how he used the facts:

> *"Then I said to them [the elders], 'You see the trouble we are in: Jerusalem lies in ruins, and its gates have been burned with fire. Come, let us rebuild the wall of Jerusalem, and we will no longer be in disgrace.' I also told them about the gracious hand of my God upon me and what the king had said to me. They replied, 'Let us start rebuilding.'"* (Nehemiah 2:17-18)

Now that's my kind of elders' meeting! Nehemiah presented the facts. The walls are in ruins (fact). The gates are burned down with fire (fact). We are disgraced among our neighbors and enemies because of the condition of our city (fact). God is gracious (fact). God prompted the king to supply all of the building materials, and they are here with me (fact). Let's build (action)! Neither Nehemiah nor the elders let the facts weigh them down.

I'm afraid I've known too many churches where Nehemiah's speech would have resulted in the formation of at least eleven committees, all of whom would have wanted oversight on data reassessment and building material reallocation. I remember sitting in a meeting at a church in Iowa where an entire hour was spent discussing the color and type of carpet that was going to be purchased. Some yelling even occurred as two particularly vocal members stood on opposite ends of the color spectrum. The best part? The meeting was tabled until the next month! The carpet was in dire need of replacing (fact). A generous donor had provided the funds to purchase the carpet (fact). A few dozen knuckleheads (fact!) were halting the progress of rebuilding because of their preferences on type and color of carpet and the belief that more facts needed to be gathered.

To paraphrase Solomon, "Of gathering many facts, there is no end…" (Ecclesiastes 12:12). When gathering data, avoid the second dream-killing obstacle that facts often provide: don't get bogged down gathering facts. Gather data; be wise, but don't let data-gathering kill the work of God in your life.

Your Assessment

Take a moment to think about the dreams God has placed in your heart. As you've been moved by Him to action and started praying powerful prayers, you've noticed the patterns of your life and the corresponding dreams He has given you. Take time to honestly assess the realities of your situation. Don't assign any value or meaning to these facts, and don't get dragged down in the endless fact-gathering process, but do establish the truth of your current endeavor.

A few months ago I got together with my good friend Eric and several other area youth pastors. For over five years, Eric has had a dream to build a multi-denominational youth outreach facility that churches would rally behind and support as a means of community evangelism. It's a fantastic dream, and God has clearly given Eric a passion for this vision. But after five years, very little church or financial support has come in, making it nearly impossible for Eric to proceed without some divine provision of God. While God has given him a clear dream, the timing hasn't been right.

While we gathered with our friend and brother around a delicious box lunch, the facts were established, and Eric could move forward based on the reality of his situation. He wasn't afraid of the facts. He didn't assess facts endlessly. He gathered information honestly, so his next move could be more clearly seen.

The facts of your situation should provide clarity to the next step of faith. Sometimes the next step is hard, aggressive and forward (like Traci and me preparing for South Africa). Sometimes the next step requires the patience of waiting for others to get on board (like Eric). Sometimes the next step is a step back to rebuild or to clarify the dream and vision. The facts help us see more clearly the direction of faith. Facts will lead us to more effective action.

What are the facts surrounding your dream?

"Friendship is born at that moment when one person says to another, 'What! You too? I thought I was the only one."
C.S. Lewis

Chapter Six
Who Are Your Friends?

While Traci and I were preparing ourselves and our family for the trip to South Africa, it was incredibly humbling to see all the people God brought alongside to make this trip a reality. One family in particular comes to mind. Daniel and Antonia Galindo don't have a lot of earthly wealth, but they are some of the richest people Traci and I are privileged to know. Their currency is love, and it would appear that their stockpile is almost endless.

The fifth principle of the *Nehemiah Project* is the principle of friendship: Surround yourself with other godly wall-builders.

Tamales for Jesus

When September of 2010 rolled around, Traci and I were about $3,500 short of our goal of $10,000 to get our whole family to South Africa. We were leaving in less than three months. It seemed that our early momentum had waned, and we were on the brink of discouragement. I remember one tear-filled night when Traci was so frustrated at the recent stop of income that she was ready to cancel the trip or at least remove the kids' tickets from the equation. I was so unfazed by the reality of our situation that I thoughtlessly ignored her concerns, and we had some real tension over the issue. I thought she was worrying. She thought I didn't care. We were both frustrated.

In stepped the Galindo family. From day one, this family longed to partner with us on the journey to South Africa, but their personal resources were even more limited than ours. Daniel's job was a little precarious at the time, and Antonia was picking up work wherever she could. They had loved on our family since they entered our church, and we had been blessed by them repeatedly and deeply.

They agreed to host a tamale sale for us. They asked that we help by taking pre-orders, and help in the kitchen on the day of the event. I have the culinary skills of a rock, but my wife is gifted and was quite the asset in the tamale-making process. The Galindos had a good friend who assisted my wife and one or two other ladies from the church, and the Galidos' two children. Together, they spent over 16 hours cooking meat, rolling and unrolling corn husks and packing in all the ingredients of their mouth-wateringly delicious tamales.

When all was said and done, they had individually wrapped over 1,500 tamales and helped us raise another $1,000 towards our trip.

The Galindos didn't go with us on our trip. They didn't board a plane; they didn't talk to one South African camper, and they didn't hold a single orphan at the orphanage. Yet they were every bit as much a part of our trip as we were! The day we came home and finally got to share with our supporters about the life-changing experience God had given our family, the Galindos were present and beaming from ear-to-ear with the joy of having shared in our adventure through their gifts and service. And they weren't alone. Many families and friends in and outside of our little church had shared in the 22,000 mile round-trip journey of our family. True community made our trip a reality.

Bricks for Jesus

Nehemiah's heart was moved. Nehemiah prayed powerful prayers. Nehemiah had dreams enlarged by his relationship with God. Nehemiah made honest assessment of the facts, but Nehemiah couldn't build the wall without the community of believers coming together — he needed other godly wall-builders.

At the end of chapter two, Nehemiah has laid out the facts of the situation and challenged the elders to join him on this massive project. They replied, *"Let us start rebuilding."* Chapter three then records the names and sometimes the social positions of the different people who helped rebuild different parts of the wall. At least twenty-eight different individuals are named, and several vocations are given, including priests, goldsmiths, rulers and perfume makers. These wall-builders came from all walks of life.

In addition to those 28 individuals, eight distinct groups are mentioned: people-groups like "the men of Tekoa", "the Levites", "the residents of Zanoah", and "the sons of Hassenaah." According to Nehemiah 5:17, 150 people ate dinner with Nehemiah each night. Obviously, a lot of people were enrolled in helping Nehemiah build the wall. Maybe a hundred? Several hundred? Nehemiah's dreams couldn't have been fulfilled without the help of fellow wall-builders.

BFFs

When I think back over God-sized stories of the Bible, I'm blown away by how God brought in the right people at the right time to see His work completed. In fact, I'm hard-pressed to think of a story where God used only an individual to do His work and not a team of wall-builders! Moses had Aaron, Jethro and 70 elders assisting him as he led the people through the wilderness between Egypt and Israel. Joshua had Caleb when they tried to convince the people to move in and take the land that belonged to the giants. When King Saul's wrath turned on David, it was Saul's own son Jonathan who stood beside David and made certain David was safe in the king's presence. Esther needed her uncle Mordecai. Ruth needed her mother-in-law Naomi and a compassionate land-owner named Boaz. Jesus surrounded Himself with three close friends and eight other fellow-servants. Paul had Timothy, Titus, Luke, Barnabas, John Mark and scores of other wall-builders. Each of these men and women accomplished great tasks for God's glory; each of them stepped off the boat and onto the water to help Jesus build His Kingdom. And each of them did it within a community of other believers.

Commentators often refer to Hebrews 11 as the "Great Chapter of Faith." All 40 verses of that chapter tell the story of faith and of the great men and women who lived extraordinary lives of service to God. Many of them might be familiar to you. Many of them may be new to you. The point of each story is that the men and women mentioned didn't settle for ordinary — they stepped out in faith and lived remarkable lives.

When you get towards the end of the chapter, the writer of Hebrews starts generalizing when he writes,

> *"And what more shall I say? I do not have time to tell about Gideon, Barak, Samson, Jephthah, David, Samuel and the prophets, who through faith conquered kingdoms, administered justice, and gained what was promised; who shut the mouths of lions, quenched the fury of the flames, and escaped the edge of the sword; whose weakness was turned to strength; and who became powerful in battle and routed foreign armies. Women received back their dead, raised to life again. Others were tortured and refused to be released, so that they might gain a better resurrection. Some faced jeers and flogging, while still others were chained and put in prison. They were stoned; they were sawed in two; they were put to death by the sword. They went about in sheepskins and goatskins, destitute, persecuted and mistreated — the world was not worthy of them. They wandered in deserts and mountains, and in caves and holes in the ground."* (Hebrews 11:31-38)

The first part of Hebrews 11 is awesome, but I wish the writer *did* have the time to tell us about these other people! Their stories of victory, even at the cost of their own lives, humble all of us who wish to be used by God. These nameless people who lived extraordinary lives and, in some cases, died extraordinary deaths did so because of their life-changing relationship with God and their desire to be more than normal.

And here's the kicker — check out the first part of Hebrews 12:

> *"Therefore, since we are surrounded by such a great cloud of witnesses, let us throw off everything that hinders and the sin that so easily entangles, and let us run with perseverance the race marked out for us."* (Hebrews 12:1)

I love the way this passage is stated in The Message:

> *"Do you see what this means — all these pioneers who blazed the way, all these veterans cheering us on? It means we better get on with it. Strip down, start running — and never quit! No extra spiritual fat, no parasitic sins."* (Hebrews 12:1)

I'll be honest, I'm not entirely sure what the author means about "Great cloud of witnesses" or "all these veterans cheering us on" (there is some good debate about it), but I love the second half of the verse that tells us to run our race. We must run with perseverance and in purity; we must run hard, and we must run striving to sin less each day. And did you catch the word "us" in his language? The writer is encouraging these believers to run together and to run with other people who are also interested in finishing the race. We must run with other wall-builders!

When Overboard Ministries began in January of 2011, my wife and I started it with the dream of publishing a book (*Project Joseph*) and maybe helping a few other guys get published, too. By April of 2011, we were already having conversations with two other authors, and, while I had just published *Project Joseph*, I was also beginning work on this book. We actually started turning some work down, as we began trying to figure out just how big this little venture was going to get.

Soon, God started opening up other possibilities, and I remember sharing some of our big dreams with a good friend.

We were hanging out, watching a baseball game on TV, when he asked about Overboard Ministries. We started talking, and before long I shared what God was doing and where I felt He was taking Overboard. I let myself get a little vulnerable, and I shared one of my big Overboard dreams — having an awesome house in a great location where my wife and I could counsel, encourage and coach other pastors and wives whose desire was to live the Overboard life. More than once Traci and I have dreamed and prayed about this idea, and in that moment I shared with him a particular property we loved and the massive price tag associated with it. I'll never forget what he said: [laughing] "That'll never happen." It was like he had just thrust a dagger in my heart; I was wounded by his words.

It was unfair of me to expect in a single moment that he should grasp all that God had been doing in my life, yet I also realized that men and women of faith understand others' faith because of their own experiences. This friend of mine loved God, but up to that point his life for the Lord had been very ordinary — he had no personal context with which to understand what it meant to step out of the comfort of the boat, to get out on the water where Jesus is building His Kingdom. In that moment, I realized that in order for Traci and me to pursue the path of Overboard living, we had to surround ourselves with others already living the Overboard life.

That doesn't mean that our dreams and goals and visions have to be shared with them — it just means that those wishing to end up like the "great cloud of witnesses" in Hebrews 11 can't build walls alone. Unlike my friend who laughed off the dream of a ministry house to bless pastors, my friends Danny, Andy, Kevin, Tim, Phil and others have never batted an eye at the price tag. They've never shrugged or laughed when we told them what God had put in our hearts and what He was doing in our lives. They've prayed with us. They've brainstormed alongside us. They've encouraged us at every turn, and, when we were settling for less, they've picked us up and reminded us of the inexhaustible goodness and grace of our God. We still believe that God has an Overboard Ministries house waiting for us — and our friends have kept us in the race.

They've done that because they, too, are in the race. They are wall-builders who understand the value of other wall-builders. Their hearts have been stirred to action. Their knees are bruised because of long bouts of powerful prayer. Their heads are filled with ginormous dreams, many of which God has already begun to fulfill. These friends know the facts and move forward, believing the grace of God is sufficient for anything they will face. And they, too, surround themselves with other wall-builders because they know the work God gives them can't be done alone.

Cherrie's Friends

While making the preparations for the first trip Cherrie would make back to the U.S. with baby Juddah, she had the distinct feeling that, with God's help, she and Juddah were going to have to take on the world. She wasn't sure how they were going to get his surgery taken care of (for his hydrocephalus); she didn't know where the money was going to come from, but she was ready to do whatever it took, even if she was alone.

However, God quickly let her know that building walls takes a community of wall-builders, and clearly Cherrie was not alone. Shortly after she landed in Virginia to visit Carilion Hospital, she started to catch a glimpse of just how big that community of wall-builders was.

The first time she was in the hospital, Cherrie was there to meet with the hospital staff with her friend Jodi and Juddah. They were trying to figure out if the hospital would help with baby Juddah's medical condition. As she walked down the hall just two minutes after arriving, Sandy, the nurse in charge, abruptly stopped, turned to Cherrie and said, "We've been praying for Juddah." Cherrie was shocked. She didn't know Sandy. They had never met. Until just a few minutes before her comment, they had never even spoken to each other. Yet she had already been taking the matter of Juddah's health before the Lord, praying powerful prayers. Sandy was a fellow wall-builder.

Later on the same visit, Cherrie walked into the N.I.C.U. to meet with Sandy and another nurse, named Nicole. Walking into Sandy's office for the first time, Cherrie looked around and her jaw dropped. Her eyes started to fill with tears, as she saw a huge picture of Juddah above Sandy's computer. Sandy saw Cherrie's response and quietly said, "We've been praying for Juddah ever since we heard about him." In fact, not just Sandy and Nicole (Cherrie had not met either woman prior to her first visit to Virginia), but half of the nursing staff on the sixth floor had become prayer advocates — prayer champions for Juddah. Cherrie wasn't alone. God had surrounded her with other wall-builders! Cherrie had a feeling Sandy would later be a part of the work in Ethiopia, and, Sandy was in fact, one of the 20-member medical group that would visit Korah in October of 2011.

Cherrie told me story after story of people who came "out of nowhere" to help her and Juddah. One of the nurses offered her house for the two of them to stay in while waiting for the various medical procedures. This nurse, Melissa, lived just three minutes from the hospital. Prior to that, Cherrie had been commuting an hour each way, several times a week. Cherrie didn't know Melissa (who also would be on the October 2011 medical trip), but she knew that God was giving her a team of helpers. Nurses offered help with clothing, fundraising, gathering donations and advocating for Juddah before the hospital administration. Today Juddah is a strong, growing and healthy little boy because, in part, Cherrie's wall-building friends made it possible for him to get the help he needed.

If you were to sit down with Cherrie over a cup of coffee and talk about Korah, she would tell you about many other people who have been a part of her incredible journey. She would tell you about her dear friend Summer, the founder of Project 61. She would tell how, from the first time they met, their hearts were knit together for the people of Korah. She would tell you about Jodi, a friend she met while both were serving in Ethiopia, and the person she and baby Juddah would first "live with" while visiting Carilion Hospital. You would hear about Vern, who facilitated Cherrie and Juddah's first speaking engagement to hospital supporters and heads of staff. She would also tell you about Nicole, one of the people instrumental in helping get Juddah to Carilion in the first place. And, of course, you would hear about Heidi, who would sacrifice her time so Cherrie could leave Juddah in Virginia and go to her daughter's graduation from Seattle Pacific University.

The list doesn't stop there. When I asked Cherrie for more names, she mentioned Wanda, who helped to facilitate the financial part at the hospital. She talked about Tim, Melissa, Hunter and Katie, who became a home-away-from-home family for Cherrie and Juddah. Then there was Mr. Martin, who went to chapel for Juddah — every day. She talked about all the sixth floor V.I.C.U. staff who continually blessed Cherrie and Juddah with gift-card donations, diapers, formula and baby clothes while in Virginia. Cherrie is quick to mention Michelle and her friends who had baby gear gathered and delivered to Cherrie's front door the day before she and Juddah arrived from Ethiopia. Then there's the His Way Fellowship family and the many prayer warriors from the blog and Facebook — too many to name. And, of course, she would mention the entire Carilion hospital staff, who donated their time and resources to help care for Juddah.

Cherrie also talks about Berhanu and Yiesmachew, who spent countless hours with her in the Ethiopian govermental offices, getting the correct paperwork done for Juddah's medical visa. The Great Hope staff in Ethiopia, who cared for Juddah and the people of Korah on a daily basis. Cherrie's husband Rick, and her children Emily, Jack and Ben, who have loved big and have not been afraid to dream big. Maleah, who invited Cherrie to go to Uganda and Ethiopia with her at the start of it all. And finally,

Beth, the reporter, who shared Juddah's journey with all of Roanoke and the surrounding area through the story she wrote.

And these names, along with those already mentioned in this story, are truly just the tip of the iceberg. Wall builders need other wall-builders.

Who are Your Friends?

Who are your close friends? When you think about your friends at school or work or church — are they wall-builders? Are they people moved by God to pray? Do they have big, God-sized dreams that they know factually are going to be tough to achieve, but, with God's help, will soon be accomplished?

If your friends are wall-builders, take some time to thank God for them and thank *them*, too. As you move forward in your own walk with God, these friends will become even closer to you, and God will accomplish great things as you all move forward, together, in your ever-deepening faith.

If your friends aren't wall-builders, maybe they just need to be asked. Many people of Nehemiah's day weren't willing to step up and do the work on their own, but when Nehemiah asked for help, they came forward and joined the cause. Some of those people in Chapter 3 had been living in Jerusalem for years, yet had done nothing to see the walls rebuilt. It took a Nehemiah to step out and call them to action. If God is moving in your heart to accomplish something great for Him, just stepping forward may be all it takes for you to see who the wall-builders around you really are.

Nehemiah 3:5 presents a very interesting contrast:

> *"The next section was repaired by the men of Tekoa, but their nobles would not put their shoulders to the work..."*

The men of Tekoa were wall-builders. The nobles of Tekoa were not. I don't know if Nehemiah argued much with the nobles or tried to convince them to work, but somehow I doubt it. He took the wall-builders who were ready to step out of the normal, and he moved forward with those who were eager to build.

I often wonder what the people like the nobles of Tekoa did when the work was done. Did they celebrate? Were they genuinely happy for the work, or did they wish they had taken part in the labor, had shared in the workload? I'm certain their joy would have been evident if they too had *"put their shoulders"* into the work.

If you don't have wall-building friends, step out in faith and see who joins you. I am confident that when we trust God, stepping out and doing what He has called us to do, He will provide who and what we need at precisely the right moments. Cherrie didn't know that God had already prepared numerous wall-builders to assist her, yet when she stepped out in faith, her fellow servants were plentiful. As the Apostle Paul so clearly states,

> *"And God is able to make all grace abound to you, so that in all things at all times, having all that you need, you will abound in every good work."* (2 Corinthians 9:8)

And again,

> *"And my God will meet all your needs according to His glorious riches in Christ Jesus."* (Philippians 4:19)

Thank God for the wall-building friends you do have and trust Him for the ones you will need. The race God has for you isn't an individual event — it's a relay, and you need other wall-builders on your team.

"Conflict builds character. Crisis defines it."
Steven Thulon

Chapter Seven
The Heat and the Hammer

Opposition is never fun. People standing up to oppose our dreams and goals can put out any fire that has been lit, and can douse any desire we have to keep moving forward in following God's plans. That internal frustration we feel when we face conflict can be a huge dream killer. More than once in my life, my inability to overcome opposition has kept me from achieving something God had laid out for me. Few people enjoy conflict, but if you want to make your life count like Nehemiah, you can be certain of the fact that conflict and opposition will be part of your journey.

Old Man Glendawn

It's important to remember, too, that we must be careful not to go out of our way to look for opposition. I'm amazed at how often some Christians sabotage their dreams by making opposition out of nothing! Sometimes the possibility of conflict *becomes* the conflict — in other words, they think they know what's going to happen, or they think they know how bad things are, so what wasn't an issue of conflict becomes just that.

When I was 20 years old, I was a summer camp counselor at a small Bible camp in western Washington. At Camp Glendawn, I worked with kids from third grade all the way through high school. It was, for the most part, a great summer.

One week, however, is forever etched in my memory because of how awful it was. I had a cabin full of third and fourth grade boys who were apparently trying out for positions in Satan's army of demons. They were an awful lot, and each one had his own special evil. Putting all eight of these guys in one cabin was particularly foolish.

Of course, I was young and arrogant, so I believed I was the Ultimate Counselor who could save these poor lads' souls. I was like Super Nanny — I would whip them into shape and have them witnessing to the homeless, giving 20% in the offering and singing "Kumbaya" by Friday night's farewell fire. Their energy plus my arrogance was the perfect formula for an explosive week of conflict.

By Wednesday, I was a puddle of misery. These 8-and-9-year-old boys had reduced me to tears, and I wasn't certain I would survive until Saturday morning when they would be picked up by their parents. However, Friday eventually arrived and with it came my friend Paul, who was joining me because he and I were off on a cross-country road trip the following morning.

With Paul's arrival, I had a renewed sense of hope and, even though I heard the boys talking about sneaking out of the cabin on the last night of camp, I was clear-headed enough to come up with a plan of action. I consulted with Paul for a few ideas, and when lights-out came for our cabin, I was ready.

We took the boys down to the lake where I told them we would share in some good old-fashioned ghost stories. They were excited by this, so we "snuck out" together as a cabin and made it to the dock. A summer fog had fallen on the lake and rolled its way up to the shore, covering part of the dock. I took all eight boys to the end of it where we began telling stories.

Their stories were lame. You could tell they were new to the whole ghost story thing, and almost all of their tales were impossible stories that ended with "True Story!" — as if saying "True Story!" somehow made the story true. After 10-15 minutes, their stories started to fade and I took over.

"Hey, you guys ever hear about what happened to Old Man Glendawn?" I proceeded to make up a story about the "founder of the camp" (no such man existed), who, of course, was a World War II vet, and had had one of his legs blown off in the war. He had a peg leg, and he loved the camp. I told the boys, "But each night, he'd wait until everyone was asleep, and then he would walk out here to the end of the dock." At this point I'd drop one foot hard on the deck making a "whump" sound, followed by dragging my other foot across the boards in an imitation of the sound of his peg leg dragging across each piece of wood. The boys were entirely caught up in my story.

I explained that Old Man Glendawn came down to the dock every night, looking off into the fog. "It was almost like he was looking *for something*. But after an hour or two, he'd just walk back and head for home. But one night..." Here I paused long enough to see that the eyes of each boy were glued to me, and I could feel the thick tension on the dock. "He never came out of the fog," I continued. "When morning came, he was gone, and no one has seen him since." Some of the guys were taking a few safety steps backward. A couple were scanning the lake as if hoping to spot him or, more likely, hoping they *wouldn't* see him!

After a couple of seconds, I finished the tale: "And on some nights, nights a lot like tonight, you can still hear the sounds of him walking on the dock." Everyone was totally quiet, holding their breath to see if tonight was one of those nights.

Right on cue, my friend Paul, who had been under the dock the entire time, brought Old Man Glendawn to life. In the silence, he struck the bottom of the dock with a broom handle, making a foot-like "whump" sound. He then dragged it along the bottom of the deck boards, creating a peg-leg-like rattling sound. It was perfect.

Eight boys simultaneously screamed, peed their pants, and sprinted for the cabin. It was one of the funniest things I have ever seen! I fell down laughing, and when I got back to the cabin, they were all buried under their blankets and sleeping bags, begging God to protect them from Old Man Glendawn. It was the only night all week that I got a good night's sleep. "True Story!"

As silly as that story is, it's not unlike the way many people create their own project-ending obstacles out of nothing. They create a bunch of "Old Man Glendawns," who are only as real as they want them to be. They give power to these possible problems and potential obstacles, and their progress gets halted by their fear. As we prepare to face down the obstacles that will come our way, let's make sure we aren't creating the problems ourselves. Obstacles are inevitable. We don't need to add any "Old Man Glendawns" to the mix.

The Apostle Paul told young Timothy, *"Everyone who wants to live a godly life in Christ Jesus will be persecuted"* (2 Timothy 3:12), and he also told him *"to endure hardship...like a good soldier of Christ Jesus"* (2 Timothy 2:3). In other words, opposition is a part of life for those wishing to step outside of their comfort zones and out into the world where Jesus is doing Kingdom work. It's not "if" it comes to opposition, it's a matter of "when." And while conflict can be a real dream killer, it can also achieve two results that are difficult to achieve any other way: first, opposition forces us to refine the vision God has given us; second, opposition pushes us back to the One who gives us the strength to persevere.

Refining Fires

The refining process isn't glamorous or glitzy. The end result is fantastic, but the process of refining is gritty work. I did some studying on ancient methods of forging and refining the blades of swords and found that the best blades went through two grueling processes, over and over.

In order to get a sword blade that is straight, sharp and strong, the swordsmith need lots of heat and lots of pressure.

When he first forges a blade, it may look good, but it's essentially an unsharp club. The blade hasn't been refined, so while it may look the part of a great weapon of war, it wouldn't stand the test in battle. Great swordsmiths take a newly forged weapon and place it back in the furnace. They get the blade as hot as possible and then pull it out and beat it with a large hammer.

Good swords have a flexible core and strong, razor-sharp edges. In order to achieve this, the swordsmith must combine varying amounts of different types of metals, and he must bond these together through the forging and refining process. More heat is applied and more pressure is delivered through each blow of the hammer.

When the forging process is complete, the weapon is repeatedly heated with intense flames from the furnace, then cooled quickly in buckets of water. The heat-treating process serves to harden the metals that have been bonded together and to prepare the blade for the sharpening process. If the metal doesn't harden, it will fracture in combat and leave its user facing certain death.

When the swordsmith has forged and treated the blade, the edges are ready to be refined to make it an instrument with deadly potential. To do this, the blade is ground down by slow-moving stone wheels, starting with large rough-cut stone wheels and ending with small, finely-cut, often hand-moved whetstones. The grinding friction against the edge slowly smooths the weapon until it is razor sharp. Then it can be matched with a hilt and given to a warrior for use in combat.

You see, without the opposition of fire and pressure, the sword would never be useful as a weapon. Take a chunk of metal and glue two pieces of wood to it, and you will perish quickly in battle. But take a chunk of metal, heat it, beat it, shape it, thrash it, grind it and refine it, and you will have a tool capable of leading an army to victory.

In the same way, our dreams and goals must be refined by the heat and pressure of opposition. Opposition applies heat to our goals; conflict delivers the pressure to forge them in clarity. As we will see, the opposition Nehemiah faced only served to clarify his vision and strengthen His commitment to trust God's hand. Like the sword that is perfected for combat through repeated heating and beating, your dreams will be refined in opposition.

Dependence on God

Not only does opposition refine our vision, but it also reminds us of how much we need to depend on God for success. It can become easy in the glow of our successes to start thinking that we are the reason for our good fortunes. We can start to believe that God is lucky to have us on His side, and, although we'd never actually say it, we begin to live like we don't need Him.

That's exactly what happened to Israel just one generation after Moses had died. In fact, God knew it was going to happen, and He gave them a stern warning in Deuteronomy 8 before Moses had left the scene:

> *"When you have eaten and are satisfied, praise the Lord your God for the good land He has given you. Be careful that you do not forget the Lord your God, failing to observe His commands, His laws and His decrees that I am giving you this day. Otherwise, when you eat and are satisfied, when you build fine houses and settle down, and when your herds and flocks grow large and your silver and gold increase and all you have is multiplied, then your heart will become proud and you will forget the Lord your God…"* (Deuteronomy 8:10-14)

Prosperity can be a killer on our spiritual journey, giving us the impression that we somehow need God less. So God allows opposition to remind us how much we must depend on Him each step of the way. Earlier in that same passage, Moses wrote this:

> *"Remember how the Lord your God led you all the way in the desert these forty years, to humble you and to test you in order to know what was in your heart, whether or not you would keep His commands. He humbled you, causing you to hunger and then feeding you with manna, which neither you nor your fathers had known, to teach you that man does not live on bread alone but on every word that comes from the mouth of the Lord. Your clothes did not wear out and your feet did not swell during these forty years. Know then in your heart that as a man disciplines his son, so the Lord your God disciplines you."* (Deuteronomy 8:2-5)

God allowed hardship and trials in Israel's progress to remind them of their absolute need to depend on the goodness and grace of God to make it to the Promised Land. They couldn't achieve the dream on their own; they had to stay intimately connected to God.

In the same way, God allows opposition in our lives to keep us close to Him. He calls it "discipline," and the writer of Hebrews tells us:

> *"No discipline seems pleasant at the time, but painful. Later on, however, it produces a harvest of righteousness and peace for those who have been trained by it."* (Hebrews 12:11)

Opposition and conflict hurt. They aren't pleasant companions on the journey, but they are necessary if we are to become all that God wants us to be, as we move forward with the dreams and plans He has established in our hearts. Opposition reminds us how much we need God, and it should move us closer to Him.

Types of Opposition

While opposition is certain, the specific type of opposition we may face is not. Nehemiah helps us see that opposition comes primarily from three different sources. These sources are unique and require us to use different tools to deal with them.

Opposition from Within

For me, dealing with conflict that comes from others is much more desirable than the conflict that comes from my own heart. There's something so debilitating when my own weaknesses and failures are exposed. Many wall-builders have faltered when confronted with their own shortcomings and sinfulness, and Nehemiah had to battle this type of opposition, too.

In Nehemiah 6, as the opposition was mounting, Nehemiah recognized what was happening: fear was beginning to take hold, and even *he* was feeling the impact of this conflict. As the pressure and heat were growing, Nehemiah started to feel afraid; he started to see his own weakness surface. I wonder if he battled self-doubt, asking questions like, "Who did I think I was to be able to lead these people to build this wall? Maybe our enemies are right, and we really can't finish this project. What will people think of me if I return to Babylon a failure?" On and on those questions could have risen, as Nehemiah was confronted with his own fear and weakness.

But look at verse nine:

> *"They were all trying to frighten us, thinking, 'Their hands will get too weak for the work, and it will not be completed.' But I prayed, 'Now strengthen my hands.'"* (Nehemiah 6:9)

Nehemiah sensed his own fear. He knew his own weakness, and it drove him back to the One who fears no one and whose strength is without limit. He knew the power of God, a God whose power is without limit and fully transferable. Nehemiah would shout "Amen" to the words of Paul,

> *"For God did not give us a spirit of timidity, but a spirit of power..."* (2 Timothy 1:7)

And the words of John,

> *"The one who is in you is greater than the one who is in the world."* (1 John 4:4)

And again with Paul,

> *"I can do everything through Him who gives me strength."* (Philippians 4:13)

Like Nehemiah before Him, Jesus faced the heat and hammer of internal opposition when Satan himself came and tempted Him. At the end of Matthew 3, Jesus was baptized, and as He came up out of the water, God spoke audibly and said, *"This is my Son, whom I love; with Him I am well pleased"* (Matthew 3:17). As Jesus' public ministry was about to start, God kicked it off by saying that Jesus was His Son and His work was very important.

Immediately after His baptism, Jesus was led by the Spirit into the wilderness, where He faced the full frontal assault of Satan. For forty days Jesus fasted and battled the enemy's temptations. Satan tried to tempt him with food, with power and with a way to fast-forward God's plan for His life. God had just said, *"This is my son,"* and Satan begins each temptation with, *"If you really are God's Son..."*

It's just like our crafty enemy to come after us internally, to get us to question the words and works of God in our lives. Self-doubt is often nothing more than an attack on what we know to be true, Satan trying to undercut the promises and sure Word of God. Notice how Jesus rebuffed each of Satan's attacks:

> *"[Satan said], 'If you are the Son of God, tell these stones to become bread.' Jesus answered,* ***'It is written:*** *"Man does not live on bread alone, but on every word that comes from the mouth of God."'"* (Matthew 4:3-4) [emphasis mine]

> *"[Again Satan said], 'If you are the Son of God, throw yourself down [from the top of the temple]. For it is written: "He will command His angels concerning you, and they will lift you up in their hands, so that you will not strike your foot against a stone."' Jesus answered him, '**It is also written**: "Do not put the Lord your God to the test."'"* (Matthew 4:6-7) [emphasis mine]

Next, the devil showed Jesus all the kingdoms of the world and made this promise:

> *"'All this [the world's kingdoms] I will give you if you will bow down and worship me.' Jesus said to him, 'Away from me, Satan! For **it is written**: "Worship the Lord your God, and serve Him only."'"* (Matthew 4:9-10) [emphasis mine]

Jesus resisted Satan's attacks by keeping the Word of God close at hand. When the enemy attacked the foundational truths of God, Jesus stood firm in His knowledge of Scripture. The internal attack was rebuffed by the true and unchanging Word of God.

The lesson is clear — we must be students of God's Word if we are going to have success overcoming the opposition from within. The enemy would love nothing more than for you and me to lose sight of God's truths. Satan and his host must party in hell every time a believer gives in to the internal opposition that causes doubts, fears and sin to put an end to God-planned, wall-building projects. Keeping ourselves closely connected to the Bible is our greatest tool against these internal assaults on the truth.

Psalm 119:9-11 reminds us,

> *"How can a young man keep his way pure? By living according to your Word. I seek you with all my heart; do not let me stray from your commands. I have hidden your word in my heart that I might not sin against you."* (Psalm 119:9-11)

So many believers try to find victory over internal opposition without the perfect Word of Truth as an aid. Hebrews 4:12 states, *"The word of God is living and active. Sharper than any double-edged sword..."* and Ephesians 6:17 states, *"Take the helmet of salvation and the sword of the Spirit, which is the word of God. With this in mind, be alert and always keep on praying..."* We are fools to undertake great deeds for God without using the weapons He has given us.

Nehemiah was armed with the promises of God and with powerful prayer as he fought the opposition that came from within. He was feeling the conflict of weariness, starting to feel the pressure of fear and tiredness, but he found help in God.

As you undertake great activities for God, you will be attacked from within. Your own flesh will try to convince you that even with God's help, you aren't able to do all that He has given you to do. The enemy will tempt you — like he did Jesus — to take a shortcut around God's plan, but, like Jesus, you must resist his attacks with the power of God's Word.

You need to memorize power passages from the Word. These are sections of Scripture that have special meaning to you because of the powerful promises they contain. They should remind you that God is in control. These passages should reinforce the idea that you are more than a conqueror because of Christ and that the enemy cannot defeat you, because he cannot defeat Christ. Below are ten of my favorite power passages, each of them committed to memory so that when the internal conflict begins, I'm armed for the battle:

Romans 8:28: *And we know that in all things God works for the good of those who love Him, who have been called according to His purpose.*

Romans 8:37: *No, in all these things we are more than conquerors through Him who loved us.*

1 Corinthians 10:13: *No temptation has seized you except what is common to man. And God is faithful; He will not let you be tempted beyond what you can bear. But when you are tempted, He will also provide a way out so that you can stand up under it.*

Psalm 119:9-11: *How can a young man keep his way pure? By living according to your word. I seek you with all my heart; do not let me stray from your commands. I have hidden your word in my heart that I might not sin against you.*

Ephesians 3:20 (The Message): *God can do anything, you know — far more than you could ever imagine or guess or request in your wildest dreams!*

1 Peter 4:7-8: *The end of all things is near. Therefore be clear minded and self-controlled so that you can pray. Above all, love each other deeply, because love covers over a multitude of sins.*

2 Corinthians 4:16-17: *Therefore we do not lose heart. Though outwardly we are wasting away, yet inwardly we are being renewed day by day. For our light and momentary troubles are achieving for us an eternal glory that far outweighs them all.*

Philippians 4:13: *I can do everything through Him who gives me strength.*

Jeremiah 29:11: *"For I know the plans I have for you," declares the Lord, "plans to prosper you and not to harm you, plans to give you hope and a future."*

Isaiah 40:30-31: *Even youths grow tired and weary, and young men stumble and fall; but those who hope in the Lord will renew their strength. They will soar on wings like eagles; they will run and not grow weary, they will walk and not be faint.*

Opposition from Friends

When you step out in faith and start living out your dreams before God, some of the most surprising opposition will come from those closest to you. This happened in Nehemiah's day, too. In one passage we see where the men of Tekoa were willing to help rebuild the wall, but the nobles of Tekoa were not. How many other friends of Nehemiah opposed this project?

Of course, one of the biggest examples of betrayal by a close friend comes from the life of our Lord Himself. On the night He was going to be handed over for His brutal crucifixion, He told His twelve closest friends that one of them was a betrayer. I can't imagine the shock and confusion that must have come over Jesus and His disciples when Judas was revealed as the traitor at their last meal together. Then, a few hours later, Judas would meet Jesus in the Garden of His first sufferings and hand Him over with the kiss of friendship. The kiss of friendship!

There is such a pain and almost indescribable agony when opposition comes from those who are closest to us. We expect it from the outside, but when it comes from brothers and sisters who should know better — that's a pain that is not easily healed. When a spouse offers scorn instead of support, or a parent turns a deaf ear to his child's cry for help, or a close friend betrays a great confidence, we feel the full force of the pressure and heat of opposition.

A few years ago I was involved in some counseling with a couple in our church. Their marriage was going through a difficult time, as both of them were trying to accomplish other ministry goals for God. As they both served faithfully in the church, their marriage looked perfect on the outside, but behind closed doors they were drifting rapidly apart.

Finally, they reached out for help and told their best friends, of their plight. Within days, this other couple had broken off all communication with them and even withdrew their kids from associating with the family. Years of friendship and sharing in children's birthday parties and family gatherings ended because of the "shock" the second family had over the troubles this couple was enduring.

The wife from the broken marriage sat in my office and sobbed. She said, "I expected a lot of people to abandon me during my struggles. But I thought 'Rachel' would stand by my side through anything. I've never felt more alone in my life than the night she turned her back on my need." Her pain was excruciating. As she tried to step out in faith and make big improvements in her marriage, opposition came from those who should have helped.

When I was a young youth pastor learning the ropes of youth ministry, I remember hurting one of my students with some careless words during her time of need. She was a young lady who had not been faithful at church, but showed up one night for youth group after being absent for many months. She hung around after we were done and obviously needed to talk. I met her out in the parking lot and asked her if everything was okay. She started to cry and then shared that during the past week, she had broken up with her boyfriend.

I was glad. He was nothing but trouble and was the main reason she had become so irregular in her church attendance. He didn't love the Lord, and I believed he had no intention of treating "Angie" with honor. As Angie shared this heartache with me, I smiled. I actually smiled. And then I remember putting my arm on her shoulder and saying, "Angie, I know this hurts, but I'm really glad the two of you broke up. It's the best thing…blah blah blah…blah blah blah…"

She didn't hear another word I spoke. She came to me to get some comfort, not a smile of happiness. She wanted someone to offer sympathy at her loss, not joy at her pain. I was glad, and I would have been lying to say otherwise, but I didn't have to express my gladness in that moment. While Angie was trying to get her life turned around after a devastating breakup with her boyfriend, I unkindly reopened the wound of her heart and applied more pressure and heat than she needed. I could have handled that situation better in so many ways and with more grace. That conversation still haunts me today.

One of the reasons opposition from our friends is so painful is that we often have to see them and interact with them after the heating and beating have taken place. Angie kept coming to church for a while, but we never had the same interactions again. The couple who came to my office needing marriage help constantly ran into their (ex) best friends. They'd see each other at the soccer field or even stand next to each other in choir. But suddenly there was a wall between them, and the hurt became a wedge that pushed them farther and farther apart.

And all too often, the person who gets wounded starts to run. The couple seeking counseling soon left our church because of the way their friends treated them. Angie took flight to another church because she never recovered from the hurt I had delivered. In fact, being young and dumb, I didn't realize it until she left our church and wrote me a letter explaining how I had hurt her so deeply. The couple never finished pursuing God's grace for their marriage — they divorced shortly after they left our church. Angie's fire for God left, and she soon found herself living for another boyfriend and settling for less than God had for her.

Certainly, both Angie and this couple could have made better decisions. Without a doubt, their spiritual collapses rest squarely on their own shoulders, but they faced opposition from those who should have been there to help. They experienced painful heat and pressure from people who claimed to love them and God, and that opposition didn't help them return to the Lord.

In both these cases, God's plan for dealing with opposition from friends was ignored. God knows we will clash with each other from time to time. He knows our sinful natures will emerge in the context of our relationships and that we will, hopefully infrequently, deliver heartbreaking words and actions. But He also provides a way for us to deal with that opposition so our relationships can be restored and progress for the Kingdom can continue. His plan is given to us in Matthew 18:

> *"If your brother sins against you, go and show him his fault, just between the two of you. If he listens to you, you have won your brother over. But if he will not listen, take one or two others along, so that 'every matter may be established by the testimony of two or three witnesses.' If he refuses to listen to them, tell it to the church; and if he refuses to listen even to the church, treat him as you would a pagan or a tax collector."* (Matthew 18:15-17)

My heart breaks when I think of Angie in light of Matthew 18. If she had come to me and confronted me with my stupidity and arrogance, I'm confident I would have confessed in that moment and sought her forgiveness (as I did later when she wrote the letter). Our relationship could have been restored, and I could have joined with her as she tried to realign her life with God's plan. Likewise, the couple aching from the loss of their friends may well have saved their friendship, and their marriage, had they followed God's plan for dealing with opposition.

Too often we take the easy road: we quit. We change our direction. We look for a shortcut. We give up. In many cases we'll do just about anything but face the opposition from our friends. But that's what the enemy wants; that's exactly what he hopes we will do. Because when our friends apply pressure and heat to our dreams and we give up, he loves to see that we have chosen a different path. He wins every time that happens.

Jesus gave us this formula for victory, a way to make sure the enemy doesn't come out on top because of our opposition. He gave us a three-step process for restoration as seen in Matthew 18.

1. Meet one-on-one, and explain the hurt to your brother or sister. By God's grace, an understanding can be reached and forgiveness can be granted and received. Problem solved.

2. If step one doesn't resolve the problem, then we must bring in two or three *godly* friends who can serve as mediators in our circumstances. These friends come as allies of peace, seeking to bring both parties together for healing. Often the wisdom of others can bring two people together so they both see their contribution to the conflict and can each seek the forgiveness of the other. Problem solved.

3. If step two doesn't resolve the problem, then church leadership should be brought in to help. By God's grace, the influence of godly church leadership can bring peace to the conflict, and forgiveness can be granted and received. Once again, the enemy is defeated.

Of course, the worst-case scenario is that even after step three, the conflict isn't resolved. According to Christ, fellowship should be broken off for the long haul until the guilty party shows the fruit of repentance. But even that is part of God's plan and vastly different from fellowship being broken because of a failure to even try to mend painful wounds.

Both Angie and the young couple severed their own friendships with the church because they chose not to follow God's plan for resolving problems. In most cases, the opposition we feel from our friends can be removed, and friendship can be restored by following the first step given to us in Matthew 18. What a shame it is when God's children don't follow God's plan for dealing with these problems!

Don't let opposition from your friends derail your work for the Lord. If you refuse to return to them to seek healing, you have failed to obey the words of Christ in Matthew 18. Not every friendship can be restored, but it's crucial that we be willing to seek restoration in obedience to God's Word. Some friends will desert you in your moments of need, just as Nehemiah was ignored by those who should have served alongside him. But seeking genuine restoration keeps the enemy at bay and prevents bitterness from destroying God's work in our lives.

Not only did we see Nehemiah overcome opposition from the nobles of Tekoa, but look at what happened to him in chapter 6:

> *"One day I went to the house of Shemaiah son of Delaiah, the son of Mehetabel, who was shut in at his home. He said, 'Let us meet in the house of God, inside the temple, and let us close the temple doors, because men are coming to kill you — by night they are coming to kill you.' But I said, 'Should a man like me run away? Or should one like me go into the temple to save his life? I will not go!' I realized that God had not sent him, but that he had prophesied against me because Tobiah and Sanballat had hired him."* (Nehemiah 6:10-12)

Opposition from our friends can be brutal, because we want to believe that those closest to us want the best for us. But as you pursue the spectacular God-sized dreams that God has put into your heart, you will face opposition from friends, and you will need to choose whether or not you will deal with it the way God instructs.

During my high school years, I was a pretty lousy brother to my little sister. She's just fourteen months younger than me, but I treated her more like the family dog than my little sis. All through high school we fought over sharing a bathroom, sharing a car and just about everything else you can imagine. It wasn't that I didn't love her, because I'm sure in the deep recesses of my heart I did. It's just that I didn't *like* her. Everyone else loved Naomi and couldn't understand my sarcasm and cruelty toward her.

Midway through my college years, God got ahold of my heart, and He burdened me for my sister. He showed me what a punk I had been and reminded me of my obligations to her as both my biological and spiritual sister. So I wrote her a letter and asked for her forgiveness for the ways I treated her in high school. I confessed openly to her and told her God was working some new things in my heart, and I wanted to be a better brother.

She's a good sis, and she forgave me. I remember when I came home that summer, we did something we had never done prior to that year — we *willingly* hung out together. One day we took a trip to the zoo and just enjoyed running around while creating some hilarious memories we still talk about.

Today, we share a good relationship with each other, our families spend time together, our kids play with one another, my sister shares in my dreams, and I share in hers. Matthew 18 played out in our lives; God was honored, Satan was defeated, and we both have been able to continue faithfully serving the Lord.

If you are facing opposition from a friend, take Matthew 18 to heart. Ask God to give you the courage to pursue restoration, so the enemy doesn't maintain the upper hand. Don't let your wall-building project get stalled or stopped because of some unresolved conflict with a friend.

Opposition from Outside

When most people think of opposition, this is the kind they generally think of. It's the more blatant and obvious form of opposition, and it's often the most "in your face." Opposition from within is subtle and tends to beat us down, day by day. Opposition from friends is often concealed with fake smiles and promises that "everything is okay," while inside someone is stewing, waiting to blow up. But opposition from the outside is usually obvious and aggressive.

When Traci and I were gearing up to host our 6.21k, we spent some time brainstorming how we might actually get runners to the event. There are hundreds of events each year in our area, and we knew that attracting a crowd would be challenging. Obviously, we had hoped the unique qualities of our race (a

6.21k on 6/21 @ 6:21pm) might be appealing, but we needed big numbers.

That year, June 21st fell on a Monday. The week before our event, my wife and I visited the park where our race would be held and took a stack of brochures to hand out to people walking and running on the trails. Our assumption was simple: if we found people using the trails on a Monday night, at about the same time our race would be held the next Monday, maybe they would join us for our event. Many walkers and runners like to participate in these types of fund raisers, so we felt certain we could create some buzz for our race.

The first 15-20 people we encountered received our brochures with enthusiasm. In fact, as it turned out, many of them actually showed up to our first race. However, after 30 minutes of passing out flyers, we ran into one couple who came walking by us near one of the playgrounds at the park. I handed the man a copy of our brochure and told him about our run. I explained that we were heading to South Africa as a family to work with students, and to do humanitarian work with orphans and AIDS patients.

The man smiled, and said that they would probably come since Monday nights were their usual night to walk at the park. However, his partner was skeptical. While the man and I were talking, she blurted out, "Wait. Is this for a church group?" I explained that I was a pastor and that some of our responsibilities would involve working with local pastors and missionaries. She grabbed the flyer from her boyfriend, crumpled it up as she handed it back, and said, "We will not be supporting the spread of religion!" Nothing else mattered to this young woman — once she heard about God, she was done.

When you start doing Kingdom work, you have to expect opposition from all sides, including — especially — those from outside your work. Granted, we can create outward opposition by ignorance, genuine mistakes or misunderstanding or even because of sheer stupidity. I was once a part of a conference for students, and for a service project, we canvassed the neighborhood asking for food donations to help a local homeless shelter. Several student groups (thankfully not our students) knocked on doors where signs were posted that stated clearly, "No Trespassing" or "No Soliciting." Not surprisingly, these students were treated poorly, sometimes excessively so, by home owners who weren't particularly pleased to be interrupted. Unfortunately, some of these kids came back and reported to the whole group their poor treatment as "persecution" against Christ, when, in fact, they had brought quite a bit of it on themselves by ignoring clear-cut parameters. Obviously, when we talk about opposition from the outside, we're talking about genuine opposition to the Kingdom work of God.

Sanballat, Tobiah and their cronies did everything they could to stop Nehemiah. They used scare tactics like playground bullies, attempting to stop Nehemiah at every turn. They threatened with physical force. They threatened with politics. They threatened with psychological warfare. They were looking for any angle they could to bring Nehemiah's construction project to a halt. They represent the third kind of opposition — the kind that comes from those "outside" our work.

These two guys and all their henchmen began their outward opposition by mocking the Jews: *"He [Sanballat] was greatly incensed. He ridiculed the Jews..."* Tobiah wasn't much nicer: *"What they are building — if even a fox climbed up on it, he would break down their wall of stones!"* (4:1-3)

It's amazing how easy it is to shrink back from a God-given task at hand because someone makes fun of us. Thankfully, Nehemiah wasn't fazed, and the Jews kept on building.

When their mocking tactics didn't work, Sanballat upped the ante by threatening physical harm: *"They all plotted together to come and fight against Jerusalem and stir up trouble against it"* (4:8). The old saying, "Sticks and stones may break my bones, but words will never hurt me" was playing out in this second threat. Since name-calling achieved nothing, Sanballat and Tobiah were ready to start chucking sticks and rocks. According to Nehemiah 4:11, they were plotting murder! But again, the Jews withstood this assault, and the building continued.

So when their first two tactics failed, Sanballat, Tobiah and several neighbors of the Jews resorted to one last form of opposition: political sabotage. They tried to arrange several meetings with Nehemiah (6:1-4), and when Nehemiah wisely avoided these gatherings, they threatened to send a message to the king that Nehemiah and the Israelites were up to no good and that a meeting with them could resolve the conflict. Of course, Nehemiah understood that *"they were all trying to frighten us"* (4:9), and this tactic also failed.

In watching Nehemiah and the Jews deal with opposition from the outside, three key principles will help us face the heat and pressure from others. First and foremost, look at what happens after each attack. In Nehemiah 4:1-3, the Israelites are mocked. In Nehemiah 4:4 we read, *"Hear us, O our God, for we are despised…"* Nehemiah prayed! Likewise in Nehemiah 4:8, Sanballat threatens physical harm and in Nehemiah 4:9 we read, *"But we prayed to our God…"* The final outward opposition takes place in Nehemiah 6:1-8, when Nehemiah again calls out to God, *"But I prayed, 'Now strengthen my hands'"* (6:9b).

Prayer is the first key to overcoming outward opposition. Psalm 69:33 reminds us that God hears the needy, He takes up the cause of those who turn to Him for help. Remember, heat and pressure drive us back to God and remind us of our need for Him. When outward opposition arises, we need to start overcoming it by going to our knees.

Planning is the second key to overcoming outward opposition. Notice that after each enemy attack, the children of Israel prayed, and then they planned. After Sanballat's first attack, Nehemiah set a goal for completing the wall to half its height.

After Sanballat's second attack, Nehemiah made arrangements for guards to watch over the builders (4:13, 16, 21), a plan for safety at night (4:22) and a distress signal to call everyone together in the event of serious trouble (4:19-20). And after Sanballat's failed third attempt at opposing Israel, Nehemiah refused to cease from his work, but persisted until the wall was finished (6:12-13, 15).

I've often found that when I follow the first step to overcoming outward opposition — prayer — the second step comes into focus. Just as reason, logic and planning aren't excuses for not exercising faith, the exercise of faith doesn't mean we give up planning. The two concepts work in harmony with each other, as we pursue the plans of God.

Clinging to God's character and nature is the third key to overcoming outward opposition. Notice in Nehemiah 4 how he rallies the troops after the second round of intimidation by Sanballat and company: *"Don't be afraid of them. Remember the Lord, who is great and awesome..."* (4:14). Nehemiah appealed to God's awesome and powerful nature as a reminder to persevere under the persecution. In chapter six he appeals to God's nature as a righteous judge when he says, *"Remember Tobiah and Sanballat, O my God, because of what they have done..."* (6:14).

The very nature of God encourages us to persist in the dreams He has given us, because the God who brought us to the point of faith to step out for His plan is able to help us finish. Paul wrote, *"Being confident of this, that He who began a good work in you will carry it on to completion until the day of Christ Jesus"* (Philippians 1:6). God's nature and character remind us to press on.

What About Your Opposition?

As you step out and pursue great dreams for the Lord, you are going to face opposition. If you are in the middle of opposition now, take some time to evaluate it in light of this chapter. (If you're not in the middle of it now, use some opposition from the past as a way to do this exercise.) Work through the following questions, thinking about the heat and pressure you are under right now:

1. List your opposition(s) on a piece of paper, and try to identify the type of conflict it represents. Is it an internal conflict? Is it conflict with a friend? Is it external? A combination of several?

2. After you've identified the type of opposition you're under, write out the ways you have tried to deal with it. Have you lashed out? Have you internalized everything? Have you just tried to ignore things? How have you dealt with your conflict?

3. Are any of your struggles internal? If so, make a list of power Scriptures that you will memorize in combating the enemy's attack on your mind. Put the power of God's Word to work in your life by committing His words to memory.

4. If you have opposition that is rooted in a friendship, commit to following God's plan for resolving that conflict. Matthew 18 gives us a means by which we can approach a brother or sister and seek restoration when our friendship has been broken.

5. Lastly, you may realize that your opposition is largely from the outside, so it's time to apply Nehemiah's three-pronged approach to gaining victory. Make it a matter of constant and intense prayer. Set specific times each day to take this matter to God. As you pray (not before!), make plans to deal with the conflict. Finally, what aspects of God's nature speak to your situation? Write out verses and stories that remind you of the nature of God and that pertain specifically to your hardships.

"There is nothing so fatal to character as half-finished tasks."
David Lloyd George

Chapter Eight
Finish the Wall

Everything in the past seven chapters is all well and good, but it means nothing if you don't apply the last principle of *Project Nehemiah*: You must finish the wall. Once you've been moved by God and compelled to act, once you've started praying powerful prayers and developed ginormous, God-sized dreams, once you've assessed facts and found other wall-building friends and are mentally and emotionally prepared for the inevitable obstacles — it's time to finish!

Nobody likes unfinished projects. You don't want a doctor doing half the surgery and calling it quits because she was hungry. I've never heard of anyone hiring a contractor to come work on a home-remodeling project and then telling him to quit half-way through the process because, "Ah shucks...looks good enough for me!" That's crazy, and that's not how people with God-sized dreams get things done.

You have to finish.

At the end of the book of Joshua, we read about the concluding years of Joshua's leadership over Israel. In his farewell speech, Joshua reminded the children of Israel, over and over, of a very important truth: The work of taking over the land wasn't finished. There was work that still needed to be done, and Joshua urged the people to finish it and not allow the remaining enemies to influence them away from the Lord. Listen to his words:

> *"The Lord your God Himself will drive them [foreign armies] out of your way. He will push them out before you, and you will take possession of their land, as the Lord your God promised you. Be very strong; be careful to obey all that is written in the Book of the Law of Moses, without turning aside to the right or to the left. Do not associate with these nations that remain among you; do not invoke the names of their gods or swear by them. You must not serve them or bow down to them. But you are to hold fast to the Lord your God, as you have until now."* (Joshua 23:5-8)

Then, in Judges, you read the story of the people taking over the land after Joshua died, and you read this statement repeatedly: *"But they didn't drive [nation x] out of their land..."* God allowed a remnant of the enemy to remain as a test for the people; Joshua knew this day was coming, so, before he died, he urged the Israelites not to fail the test. They needed to finish. Look at these accounts in Judges:

> *"The Lord was with the men of Judah. They took possession of the hill country, but they were unable to drive the people from the plains...The Benjamites, however, failed to dislodge the Jebusites...But Manasseh did not drive out the people of Beth Shan or Taanach or Dor or Ibleam or Megiddo...Nor did Ephraim drive out the Canaanites...Neither did Zebulun drive out the Canaanites...Nor did Asher drive out those living in Acco or Sidon or Ahlab or Aczib or Helbah or Aphek or Rehob... Neither did Naphtali drive out those living in Beth Shemesh or Beth Anath...The Amorites confined the Danites to the hill country..."* (Judges 1:19, 21, 27, 29-31, 33-34)

The Children of Israel failed the test — they didn't finish. The outcome was disastrous: "[*The angel of the Lord said*], *'Now therefore I tell you that I will not drive them out before you; they will be thorns in your sides and their gods will be a snare to you'*" (Judges 2:3). And before Chapter 2 is finished, we read this ominous passage: *"Then the Israelites did evil in the eyes of the Lord and served the Baals. They forsook the Lord, the God of their fathers, who had brought them out of Egypt. They followed and worshiped various gods of the peoples around them…"* (Judges 2:11-12)

When you have seen the principles from Nehemiah's life play out in the way God has led you to and through a project, you must finish. Nehemiah didn't stop when the wall was halfway done (Nehemiah 4:6); he worked until every last brick and piece of stone and massive piece of timber was set in place. *"So the wall was completed…in fifty-two days"* (Nehemiah 6:15). God had moved. Nehemiah prayed. God had provided. Nehemiah finished.

One of the biggest problems with quitting a project is that our choice to quit assumes our knowledge of how it would have ended. Thomas Edison once said that many of life's biggest failures are people who quit without knowing how close they were to success. It's relatively easy to start well, but finishing is something entirely different. There are obstacles to overcome. There are challenges to rethink. There are people telling you how silly you are for trying and how smart you'd be for "living like everyone else." There are painful lessons to learn. All of these pressures make quitting the easy choice, but quitting is not an option for those pursuing the path God has laid out before them.

Cherrie Didn't Quit

Cherrie had a lot of reasons to quit her work with the hurting and hungry in Ethiopia. A lot of voices gave her good reasons to stop the work that God had put in her heart. After all, what could *one* person really do to make a difference? Is it reasonable that she and Rick could help little baby Juddah with his hydrocephalus and other medical conditions? Would anyone listen to Cherrie as she expressed her passions for Ethiopia? Could one person really change anything? Even Cherrie has felt overwhelmed by the needs in Korah. Look at a blog post she updated in December of 2011:

I returned on Friday from my eighth trip to Korah, Ethiopia. My good friend Kathleen and I were team leaders on a medical missions team where we set up a mobile clinic in Korah and at the boarding school in Shashamane. Our team consisted of 21 members. We saw and treated over 150 patients a day.

In my mind, I thought this trip would be similar to the other times I have been in Korah. My eyes would be opened to a different way of life, and, as I grew in relationships with my friends in Korah and learned from them, God would guide and direct where we could work together to improve lives and share the love of Jesus. Together we would work to make changes for the good in Korah, in the "here and now" and in the Eternal. As with most who enter Korah, the blessings received far outweigh the blessings we leave behind. There is much to be learned from Korah.

Generally, I'm not a crybaby while in Korah. I'm able to contain myself and not let my emotions overtake the moment. With God's help, I have been able to be *in* the moment, without being overcome *by* the moment. Until this trip, I remember just one devastating moment in Korah where the floodgates opened and tears fell uncontrollably. It was the day a 14-year-old girl hung herself just three doors down from the shelter. She had been sick for a week and thought she would not recover. It's always been at night when I return to my bed, and I let my emotions go and give way to the gut-wrenching thoughts and pain of all the "what if's" and the "why, God?" questions that come from being submerged into Korah, and that's when the tears fall.

This trip was not like that. Numerous moments during this trip I found myself unable to contain my emotions. My body and my mind gave in to the sadness and depths of despair, and a never-ending ache overtook my soul. It was like I was in a dream. And this was a trip that was like no other.

On one of the evenings in the beginning of our trip, as our team sat in the gathering room of the guesthouse, Kathleen and I asked each team member to summarize his or her feelings about the first day in Korah in one or two words. Again, at the end of the trip we asked them to share what their first word was at the beginning of the trip and what their word was now, after spending 10 days there. It was interesting to hear how team members' words changed from words that expressed sadness to words that expressed joy and happiness. To my surprise, my words went the opposite direction. My first words were something along the lines of reunion and joy. My last two words were:

"Complicated desperation."

Yes, those sum it up accurately. Complicated desperation. Complicated: made up of intricate parts or aspects that are difficult to understand or analyze. Desperation: recklessness arising from despair.

Korah is difficult to understand, and I wonder if there will ever be a way to fully understand or analyze it. Korah is made up of a million different moving intricate parts. Recklessness is obvious, arising out of the despair, which is most evident when you start to focus on scars that have formed on the skin of the residents, and they begin to share their personal stories of how the scars came into being. Heart scars which affect relationships are tangible, surrounding you everywhere you go in Korah. Korah is a perplexing place, and the more times you visit, the pieces begin to fall together, and the more you think they are falling together, you realize that only the surface has been scratched, and there are a million more pieces needing to be investigated.

Complicated desperation. I felt it pierce so deep into my soul this trip that I wasn't sure if I'd be able to come out on the other side. I wasn't directly involved in the following situations; I was just a bystander present in the moment.

It was one day in clinic, toward the end of the day. A mother brought her young daughter into the clinic. The baby lay limp in her arms. She was brought to the station of a team member, a pediatrician and surgeon from Uganda. As Dr. Arlene examined her, the diagnosis was not promising. As the young mother began to share the history of this small baby, my heart quickly dropped. I could feel the weight of this mother's agony on my shoulders, and my spirit fell hard.

The baby, now two years old, had reached all the normal milestones by the age of 1 1/2. She was walking, talking and crawling. Then just six months ago, the baby had a fever and quickly began to regress to the point she was now. Unable to sit, walk, crawl or do anything on her own. She lay in her mother's arms just as a newborn baby. As Dr. Arlene continued to examine her, she felt the baby had contracted meningitis, and this was the reason for her decline. But as the examination and conversation continued, something much closer to home was revealed. This baby also had hydrocephalus and fused sutures. Her "sunset-eyes" were a tell-tale sign that her inter-cranial pressure has begun to increase, and most likely she had started to have headaches similar to migraines. Her head circumference was much too large for her age. As the doctor listened to her heart, it was quite clear that she also had a heart condition. My thoughts immediately went to Juddah and the day I first held him in my arms and realized that something was not quite right with his head. And then to his diagnosis day of hydrocephalus and fused sutures. And then to the day when the doctor at the Ethiopian hospital told me to "let him go. They can't do anything for him."

It was like in a movie where you see your life flash before you in fast forward. This baby was a lot like Juddah. And now here, we, as a team, are in the presence of a two-year-old with the same condition as Juddah, and we have nothing to offer her. NOTHING. Not even a hospital or doctor to refer her to that could offer the possibility of a future. Nothing that will help her baby get well. Nothing that will help her baby survive. Nothing that will help reverse this horrible condition that has overtaken her little body. Nothing to bring back the little girl she remembers just six months ago. Questions ravage my mind, not solutions. Maybe if the baby were younger? Maybe if the baby didn't have a heart condition. Maybe if the baby had been born in the USA. Maybe... but maybes didn't and don't matter here... We have to live in the facts of what is, not in the maybes of what could have happened. I felt as though I couldn't breathe. I can't even begin to imagine how this mother of this fragile baby continues to courageously go on. The moaning and tears that came from this young mother's belly were indescribable.

Keena, a team member who was sorting and distributing clothes to patients, was busy picking out a new set of clothes to give to the mama for her baby. She had several new outfits picked out ready to give her. As Keena handed them to me, I couldn't help but think that we were giving the mama new clothes that her baby would be buried in. Oh, sweet Jesus, please don't let my mind go there. But it did. Most likely this baby will not survive to her third birthday due to her heart

> condition, hydrocephalus, the poverty and the infections she will acquire from her surroundings in Korah. Dr. Arlene wrote out an extensive report to a doctor we have a connection with at Brooke Hospital in Addis. The doctor there may be able to prescribe some medication that would help slow the production of CSF fluid and help with some treatment that would minimally prolong her life. Due to this baby's age and progression of her condition, no hospital would even begin to entertain the idea of lifesaving treatment for her. And the tears fell. Uncontrollably and unstoppable.
>
> We had nothing. WE HAD NOTHING. But we serve the one who has everything. Our Jesus has everything. So we prayed over and with this mama and her baby. We gave her some money to purchase formula for the baby and to cover the costs of going to Brooke Hospital. I hugged her hard, not wanting to let her go. It was apparent from the deep sorrow that fell from this mother's eyes that she was well aware the prognosis was not good.

So what could one person do against all of this? How could one person change this outcome? One person can't, but one person can be the reason that hope arises from the ashes of despair. It takes just one person to step out of the comforts of this life and out into the storms where God is working powerfully, to see eternal changes ripple through homes, communities, cities, states and nations! Like a rock thrown into the middle of a calm Cherrie has jumped out of a comfortable boat, and the ensuing ripples are changing lives for eternity.

Just this last week a Christmas benefit concert was hosted for the people of Korah here in Salem. Close to 100 people were in attendance to help raise funds and awareness for the plight of the people in Ethiopia's most deprived community. Presently, a team of people on both coasts of our country are actively supporting the work that Cherrie is a part of. Salem, Oregon, and Roanoke, Virginia, both regularly send teams and raise funds to join this ministry of saving lives in Korah.

Today, Cherrie's eldest child is four months into a year-long commitment to live and serve in Korah. Baby Juddah is 14 months old and is alive, living with Rick and Cherrie, because people have helped cover his medical needs, including extensive surgeries, travel expenses and countless doctor visits. In October of 2011, over 20 people joined Cherrie on a 10-day medical missions trip, seeing over 150 patients every day. Today, Cherrie has teamed up with Project 61 to see more help and aid come to Korah. Today baskets and jewelry are made in Korah and sold through an online store, making life-changing resources available, especially to the women and children of Korah. Today, a young man named Sammy is visiting America, sharing how his life has been changed by the love of God and by people like Cherrie; he is raising awareness and support for the work in Ethiopia. Today there is hope in Korah. Today, even while you read this sentence, God's love is saving people physically and spiritually in Korah.

Cherrie didn't quit when the enemy presented many opportunities for her to do so. Others had come and been overwhelmed. Just the despair found in Korah would have been enough for almost anyone else to call it quits. but not someone like Nehemiah — not Cherrie. Cherrie is a finisher.

Finish Strong!

Few of us "old folks" will ever forget the amazing story of the Olympic runner Derek Redmond. In the Barcelona Olympic Games of 1992, Derek was a competitor in the men's 400m dash, and it was believed by many that he would win the gold. His injury-plagued career seemed to finally be behind him, and, as the current world-record holder entering Barcelona, this was *his* year. As the race began, he started fast, and at the 200-meter mark, he was making his move, creating some separation from the other runners when the unthinkable happened — Derek pulled up lame. He had torn a hamstring. He collapsed on the track.

The packed-out stadium was disappointed for Redmond. As the other racers finished, many fans were still watching Redmond's huddled mass on the track. As they watched, Derek stood up at the 250-meter mark and started walking/skipping/hopping his way towards the finish line.

Every step was agonizing. Derek winced with each pace, and, after another 50 or so meters, few thought he could finish, but he persisted. Security guards came to assist him, but he waved each one off. Fans started cheering him on, hoping against all hope that he could reach the end.

Derek had made a decision in his heart — he was in the Olympics, and he was going to finish! Nothing would keep him from completing this race. Suddenly, Redmond got up and started to run. Only it wasn't Derek Redmond running — it was his dad, Jim Redmond, who had broken through security to get next to his son on the track. In what many remember as one of the most touching scenes in sports history, Jim put his arm around his son, and the two of them started toward the finish line together.

Realizing his father was going to help him make it, Redmond buried his head in his father's arm and began to sob. With his dad's help, Derek finished the 400-meter event, to the roar of the crowd — a roar many times larger than the gold-medal victor had received. Derek Redmond overcame incredible obstacles. He didn't quit. He didn't surrender. He didn't walk off the track in shame or disappointment. He finished strong.

You must finish what God has laid out before you. Opposition will arise. Reasons will abound as to why you should quit, but you must not relent from what God has put in your heart to do. When you've seen principles 1-6 come together in your God-sized dreams, you must throw off the temptation to stop before God's work is done. You must complete the task.

The author of the book of Hebrews begins his wrap-up with these words in Chapter 12: *"Let us run with perseverance, the race marked out for us..."* (Hebrews 12:1). God has given your race to you, and He has given you everything you need to run it. *"His divine power has given us everything we need for life and godliness"*, writes Peter (2 Peter 1:3), and his words remind us that when God brings us to a great task, He has also given us everything we need to finish!

Don't pull up short. Don't stop because others have zoomed by you. Don't quit because the obstacles seem too big. Don't allow the magnitude of the project to bring despair and hopelessness. Like Nehemiah, you must step out and let God's greatness shine through you.

Nehemiah didn't finish the wall because of how awesome *he* was — he finished because of how awesome *God* is! Cherrie hasn't facilitated an amazing work in Korah because *she* rocks — she has seen an unbelievable dream become reality because *God* rocks. Peter didn't walk on water because of his own power over nature — he walked on water because the Creator of water empowered him to do so.

None of the following people did what they did because of their own greatness — they did what they did because of God's greatness: Paul traveled and spread the Gospel throughout all of Europe, the Middle East and parts of Russia and Asia; Noah built a boat and literally saved humanity; Deborah brought about victory where defeat was certain; a demon-possessed man experienced healing and then became a missionary to ten key gentile cities; Daniel ate a special diet and grew in wisdom and physical appearance greater than those around him (eventually an entire kingdom would know of Daniel's God); Esther saved Israel from genocide. On and on, all of these individuals finished what they started, and, in so doing, the greatness of God poured out through their work.

You, too, can experience the power of God, so don't pull up short. You must finish!

Are You Finishing Strong?

Do you have a finishing mindset? Are you, like Nehemiah, like Cherrie and like Derek Redmond, ready to finish the race God has put before you? Here are a few other questions to answer:

1. Are there any unfinished tasks in your life that you need to go back and complete? Did God move in you to get a task started, yet some opposition (internal, external, from friends, etc.) caused you to turn from the path? Identify that task and set a plan to see it finished.

2. Often we don't know the timeline for finishing a project. I doubt Nehemiah knew the wall could be built in fifty-two days, but he set out on the task and ordered his life in such a way that the project could be completed. What lifestyle changes do you need to make in order to see your goals achieved? Do you need to change your freetime habits so the work God has given you can have access to more of your calendar? What daily/weekly changes could you make to give yourself the time and energy needed to see the work God has given you come to completion?

3. Who in your life will hold you accountable to achieving the goals God has given you? Do you have someone who will keep your feet to the fire through encouragement, confrontation (when necessary) and prayer? If so, enlist him or her to help you. If not, pray for a friend like that. Step out in faith and see who God brings to your aid.

"People are more important than puppies."
AJ Castañeda

Chapter Nine
People, Not Projects

I'm a people person. Give me the choice between a party with people or working alone on a project for hours, and I'll take the people every time. I enjoy projects, too, but usually because they help connect me with people. I know not everyone is wired this way. Some of you reading this are project-people. You like hanging out and being around your friends, but your preference is to work on things. You like tasks, and you get fired up when a challenge is laid out before you where you can make charts and diagrams, or you can jump right in and start using your hands. You are project-people. I am people-people.

Whether you have a natural bent towards projects or towards people, one last truth remains for those wishing to take on big things for the Lord: We must not forget about the people involved. Even — maybe especially — when we're up to our eyeballs in project details, we must remember the people behind these projects. Whether it's building a well in a drought-stricken part of the world or fixing a meal for a needy neighbor, people will populate God's Kingdom, and we can't lose sight of the souls.

VBS, Soccer Camp, and Kidnappers

A few years ago I led my students on back-to-back-to-back mission trips. We spent the first week in Philadelphia, working with homeless people in one of our country's toughest neighborhoods. It was a grueling week of ministry, but a great way to kick off our summer missions focus.

We flew in from Philly on Saturday, met at church on Sunday morning, and on Sunday afternoon we headed south near Eugene, Oregon. That week we worked with a sister church, helping them hold a soccer camp outreach by day and youth outreaches by night. It was an awesome time of sharing God's love through sport and helping them develop a ministry to reach students for Christ.

When our last day of camp was over on Friday, we headed home and met back at our church Sunday night to begin our final week of ministry at home. Already it had been a good two weeks, but we were all starting to feel a little weary. Our last week was a mission trip to our own town, where we would lead a soccer camp and VBS at our own church, while organizing a peer-to-peer outreach for the weekend.

As the soccer camp began on Monday, we had a big turnout from the community — lots of visitors and children came in from the neighborhood. Our high school students, twelve in all, did a great job of leading the event, and, when we finished at noon, everything was off to a great start. Or so I thought.

A 12:05, when I hopped out into the parking lot to see how things were going, I noticed 11 of my 12 students were in a circle talking to each other, while more than 40 soccer kids were running around wild. Parents were picking up kids from the front lawn (a football field away from where our students were "watching them") and throughout the parking lot. It was a horrible scene. I took a picture to show them as an object lesson, moments before one of the parents caught my arm.

This mom, "Carol," was one of our neighbors. She was a sweet woman, and two of the kids present were from her daycare. These kids were at our program, and their parents were going through the wringer. She told me that the kids' mom and dad were in fierce legal and custody battles and that one of the parents was trying to pick up the kids any way they could, even defying court orders to the contrary. When Carol came to pick them up, she was dismayed to find them climbing trees right next to the street, easily accessible to the parent who was trying to, essentially, kidnap them from the other parent. She laid into me, and she was right. We had failed to remember the kids.

That afternoon is one that many of those 12 high school students will never forget. In fact, if some of them are reading this section now, I'm confident they have that sick feeling in the pit of their stomachs just as we all did the day we "discussed" it. Okay, it wasn't much of a discussion.

When all the soccer kids had been picked up, I had my students grab their lunches and come to the auditorium where we would debrief. I let them eat for a while, but I was stewing. I had been pretty amped up when I took the picture; I became angry after Carol explained the gravity of the situation.

I let them eat for about 15 minutes, when I turned their attention to my iPhone and had them look at the picture I had taken from the end of the day. I wanted them to see it up close and personal. After it had been passed around to everyone, I asked them the simple question: "What do you notice about that picture?" JJ was one of the first who responded: "We are all together in a circle and there are no kids with us." Indeed.

I blasted them for the next 20 minutes, telling them about my conversation with Carol. I reminded them that it's *people* that matter, not projects. It wasn't enough to just complete a day of soccer camp and VBS: we had to invest in people. If we completed the week of events, but failed to minister to people — we failed all the way around! However, if we managed to minister to people, but failed to complete soccer camp — we could still hold our heads high and know that we had been involved in Kingdom Work. The project was important, but only because it gave us an opportunity to minister to *people*.

Each of those students took it hard. They hung their heads like the family dog does after it gets yelled at for peeing on the carpet. It wasn't a fun day. When one of my students graduated a few years after that, she told me, on the night of her graduation, "The worst day of my youth group experience was that day at VBS. It still makes me sick to think about what could have happened when we lost sight of what was important." It was a painful, but valuable, lesson we learned that day. We cannot allow projects to become more important than people.

People, Not the Wall

In the midst of Nehemiah's work for the Lord, a dispute broke out about people. In chapter five, Nehemiah became aware of the problem of Jews exacting steep interest and collateral from loans they had provided to their Jewish brothers. The king of Babylon was charging heavy taxes, and, in order to pay them, some of the Jews had to borrow money from other Jews so the king would be satisfied. The result was that some in Jerusalem had already lost all their land and holdings, as well as some of their children, to others who were relentless in taking more than was necessary. All of this was being done by Jews, against other Jews, and was a violation of God's clear command:

> *"If you lend money to one of my people among you who is needy, do not be like a moneylender; charge him no interest. If you take your neighbor's cloak as a pledge, return it to him by sunset, because his cloak is the only covering he has for his body."* (Exodus 22:25-27)

So Nehemiah stopped his work on the wall and jumped in to help the people. Even though this massive construction project was all-consuming, he took the time to keep first things first. Nehemiah stopped progress and listened to the complaint of the people (Nehemiah 5:1-5).

It would have been so easy to say, "Look, in case you didn't notice, I'm kind of busy right now. I'm building the wall that's been neglected for a long time, and, in fact, building this wall is actually going to help *you*. So if you all could just figure out your own solutions, I'd be very grateful!" But he didn't. He stopped his work and took time to hear about the injustices against his brothers and sisters.

Listening wasn't enough, though. Once Nehemiah realized what was going on, he crafted a plan of action. Nehemiah 5:7 says, *"I pondered [the charges] in my mind...."* Nehemiah knew he needed to act, but first he formulated a plan. Maybe he took time to interview others to confirm the charges. Maybe he just paced back and forth on a section of completed wall while weighing his options. Whatever it was, he put his plan together, so the people could be helped.

Nehemiah listened. Nehemiah crafted a plan. Finally, Nehemiah acted on what he had heard: *"Then [I] accused the nobles and officials"* (Nehemiah 5:7). Nehemiah took the matter to those who were guilty, and he laid out the charges before them. Following the principles of confrontation, he went right to the source and presented the offending parties with truth and grace. He told them the gravity of the matter and then gave them a clear path to be restored.

The nobles responded to Nehemiah's plea, and they chose to follow God's path, not theirs. The priests came and solidified their commitment to return the money and property taken in violation of God's commands, and Nehemiah was seen as a humble and gracious leader who kept *people* at the heart of all he did. Even though he was eating, sleeping and drinking "the wall," he never forgot that every project is ultimately about people. The Jews honored him by making him governor of the region for the next twelve years, and he served God with the same continued grace and humility (Nehemiah 5:15-19).

People, not Projects

As you move forward in the plans God has put on your heart, don't forget the people who will be impacted and changed by what you do. It's so easy to become driven to finish that we forget about the people along the way. Nehemiah didn't lose sight of first things. Yes, the wall needed to be built. Yes, stopping to solve the problem of usury took up time that could have been invested in building. Yet, through it all, Nehemiah teaches us that projects and people go hand in hand, just as faith and planning join together in God's path for our lives.

Here are three ways to help you remember that projects should serve people, and not the other way around:

1. *Pray for people.* In our eagerness to see God do great things through our work, it's easy to pray for the project and for people to finish their work, but to forget to pray for the people. Take time to pray for the needs of the people you are serving, working with, or working for. Pray for their families. Pray for their jobs. Pray for their hearts to grow in faith and grace as they serve the Lord.

2. *Look around.* Sometimes our heads can get so buried in our work that we don't realize what's happening right next to us. I used to harass a friend of mine who is one of the most diligent and focused people I know. I once walked into his office while he was working on a project and tried to interrupt him. Immediately, I realized my timing was bad, and he, understandably, wasn't hearing a word I said. I started to leave his office and casually said, "So, I'm just going to go and jump off the bridge. Cool?" to which he said, "Sounds good." (I should have added that he owed me a few million dollars — he would have agreed to anything!) I laughed and stepped outside, knowing that I do the same thing to others when I get immersed in a project. Take a second to breathe, stand up and look around, and you might be amazed at what you see just by looking up.

3. *Ask for help.* I'm surrounded by people who help me stay on track. I have friends who will call me out when I've crossed the line, making things or projects more important than people. Ask for help from others, and ask them to be an extra set of eyes for you. Make sure you

trust these people and that they love God first — they'll become a lifeline for you as you tackle the great works God gives you. Make sure these people know you well and that they are willing to ask hard questions and give tough advice. More than once, my friends have saved me with a simple question like, "If I asked Traci how you're doing in taking time for her, what would she say?" That one always makes me think, and it always makes me grateful for the friends in my life who care enough to be tough when I need it.

"No one lives long enough to learn everything they need to learn starting from scratch. To be successful, we absolutely, positively have to find people who have already paid the price to learn the things that we need to learn to achieve our goals."
Brian Tracy

Chapter Ten
Start Building

The seven principles from the life of Nehemiah can be applied to your life and mine — today! We can take each of these seven concepts and put them into practice as we tackle great things for God. It might be that you are already partway through a project, needing to apply some of these principles in order to finish. Maybe you've felt God's leading in your life to take a serious step of faith, but you just haven't known how to get started. Wherever you are in the process, applying these principles will create forward progress in completing your God-given dreams.

Principle #1: Let your heart be moved by God.
Nehemiah reminds us that dreams and goals are formed when we allow our hearts to be moved by God. This requires sensitivity to His Spirit, to His Word and to the consciences He has given us. When we live in tune with what God is doing, our passions will be stirred to respond to injustice, to meet needs, to help the poor, love the lost and build the Body. Our dreams begin when our hearts and minds are sensitive to God.

Principle #2: Pray powerful prayers.
When God starts shaking things up in your life, start praying powerful prayers that depend entirely on Him. Don't pray for half — pray for God to do what only He can do: the impossible! Pray passionate, persistent prayers that are God-focused and depend on His power for answers. If God is behind your

dreams, His power needs to be behind your work. And make sure prayer is a regular part of your daily work.

Principle #3: Dream ginormous dreams.
Nehemiah dreamed about rebuilding an entire wall, complete with gates and guard outposts. He dreamed that the king might have a part in providing *all* of the building materials and even offering safe travel to and from the job site. His powerful prayers led him to ask for help from a person who, from all realistic viewpoints, was highly unlikely to help.

Principle #4: Take honest assessment.
Take time to look at the facts of your situation. Remember, facts and faith work hand in hand, but it's good to know where things stand before (and during and after!) we begin our God-sized projects. However, don't let facts bog down the work of faith, and don't make the mistake of assigning meaning to the facts. Nehemiah inspected the wall and saw that things were in sad shape. That fact didn't change his work; it just allowed him to approach it with a clear plan. We need facts, *but facts never trump faith.*

Principle #5: Surround yourself with other wall builders.
Wall builders need other wall builders to help them finish what God has put in their hearts to do. So many of the great men and women of the Bible did what they did because of the people God graciously put into their lives. Nehemiah needed an army of other builders, and God granted him just that. Find godly friends who are often moved and know how to pray powerful prayers. Surround yourself with individuals who dream big, can assess facts and want to be with other wall builders themselves. Build friendships with people who know how to handle opposition and who keep *people* in mind while finishing projects.

Principle #6: Prepare for opposition.
You *will* face opposition; be ready. Opposition will come from three main sources and each of them must be dealt with in its own unique way. (1) Opposition from within can be combated

with the power of God's Word. (2) Opposition from friends can be handled according to God's blueprint for conflict management. (3) Opposition from without can be resolved through prayer, planning and total reliance on the character and nature of God.

Principle #7: Finish the dream.
We must be finishers. At the end of the day, as we follow the lead of God, we must follow it to the end. That doesn't give us permission to neglect people along the way, but, rather, to be mindful that projects serve people. As we finish what God has given us to do, we are truly ministering to others with our labor.

The Next Nehemiah?
Are you ready to be the next Nehemiah? Maybe it's a neighbor who needs to be reached for the Lord, or maybe it's an orphanage in India that needs to be built. Maybe God is working in your heart to start a ministry to the homeless in your hometown, or maybe He just wants you to reach out to one homeless man on a street corner and offer him friendship. Maybe it's an entire community in Africa that can be impacted by your labors of love and mercy, or maybe the project God has for you is to help build a community garden that will give you the ability to witness to neighbors.

It's not the size of the project or task that God gives us that matters; it's the willingness in our hearts to be used by Him to advance His Kingdom. Follow the seven principles in the life of Nehemiah and watch what God will do through you.

Are you ready to start building?

About the Author

Joe Castañeda has been in full-time Christian ministry for over 16 years, the past 15 as a youth pastor in two different churches. He married his high school sweetheart, Traci, and together they've had three children during their fifteen years of marriage.

He did his undergrad work at Faith Baptist Bible College in Ankeny, Iowa, where he received a B.S. in Pastoral Ministry with emphases in counseling and Christian education. For the past 12 years he has been working diligently on his M.A. in youth ministry (he assures us that cramming a two-year degree into 12 is no easy task). His studies began at Northwest Baptist Seminary in Tacoma, Washington (now Corban School of Ministry), and have continued for the last eight years through Western Seminary in Portland, Oregon.

Joe's first book, *Project Joseph,* was the first in the Life Improvement Series, and he has plans for at least one more in that set.

Today, Joe continues to write at www.tenthdotministries.com, an online daily devotional site he writes with friend and world-class illusionist and communicator, Danny Ray. He also writes devotional material aimed at helping students and parents come together around the Word of God, through special ten-day experiences. Find out more at www.the10dayjourney.com.

In January of 2011 he founded Overboard Ministries, the umbrella ministry for much of his writing and speaking. You can find more information about Joe and his ministry, including ways to contact him, at www.overboardministries.com.

Who or What is Overboard Books?

Overboard Books publishes quality books that are designed to assist in getting Christians overboard — out of the boat. It's the publishing arm of Overboard Ministries, whose mission is based on Matthew 14. In that chapter we find the familiar story of Jesus walking on water, while His disciples were in a boat. It was the middle of the night, the water was choppy and Jesus freaked out His followers who thought He was a ghost. When they realized it was Him, Peter asked to come out to Him on the water, and he actually walked on top of the water like Jesus.

But what truly captivates me is the thought of the other eleven disciples who remained in the boat. I've often wondered how many of them questioned that move in the years to come. How many of them wished they hadn't stayed in the boat, but had instead gone overboard with Peter? Overboard Ministries aims to help Christians get out of the boat and live life for Christ out on the water where He is building His Kingdom. We hope and pray that each book published by Overboard Ministries will stir believers to jump overboard and live life all-out for God, full of joy, and free from the regret of "I wish I had..."

What We Do

Overboard Books is the publishing arm of Overboard Ministries. Overboard Ministries emerged in the summer of 2010 as an umbrella ministry for several concepts my wife and I were developing. One of those concepts was a book ministry that would help other Christian authors get published. I experienced a lot of frustration while passing my first manuscript around. I kept getting rejection letters that were kindly written, but each echoed the same sentiment: "We love this book. If you were already a published author, we would love to publish it." They were nice letters, but that didn't make the rejection any easier or the logic less frustrating.

Out of that came the audacious idea to start our own "publishing company." I put that in quotes because I want people to know a couple of things. First of all, we're not a traditional publishing company like most people envision when they hear the name. We don't have a printing press in our garage, and we don't have a marketing team. Basically, we're a middleman who absorbs most of the front-end costs of publishing in order to help you get published, while making sure the majority of profits end up in your pocket, not ours.

Our desire is to keep costs to a bare minimum for each author. (As of this writing, there is only a minimal contract fee when your manuscript is accepted.) We provide resources and ideas to help authors work on marketing, while also providing the editor and graphic design artist at our expense. We subcontract out the printing, which speeds up the time it takes to move from final draft to bound book. Since we don't have much overhead, we can keep our expenses low, allowing seasoned authors, or first-time authors like me, the opportunity to profit from their writing. This makes it possible for authors to publish more books while continuing in their current jobs or ministries.

Contact Us
If you are interested in other books or learning about other authors from Overboard Books, please visit our website at www.overboardministries.com and click on the "Overboard Books" link. If you are an author interested in publishing with us, please visit our site and check out the "Authors" tab. There you will find a wealth of information that will help you understand the publishing process and how we might be a good fit for you. If we're not a fit for you, we'll gladly share anything we've learned that might be helpful to you as you pursue publishing through other means.

Thank You
Thanks for supporting our work and ministry. If you believe this book was helpful to you, tell someone about it! Or better yet, buy them a copy of their own! We completely depend on word-

of-mouth grassroots marketing to help spread the word about Overboard Ministries and its publications. Please share our website with others and encourage them to purchase the materials that will help them live "overboard" lives for Christ. Also be sure to visit our blog, easily accessible from the Overboard Ministries website, and, while you're there, sign up for our e-mail list.

May God bless you as you grab the side of the boat, take a deep breath…and jump onto the sea!

Joe Castañeda
Founder, Overboard Ministries
Lifer, Striving To Live Overboard

Other Overboard Ministry Books

Project Joseph: By Joe Castañeda

Project Joseph was the first title published by Overboard Ministries. *Project Joseph* helps people walk through the pain of their past, using principles from the life of Joseph in Genesis, so its readers can experience true healing from God. Many times it's our hurts and pains that keep us in the comfort of the boat instead of being on the water where Jesus is building His Kingdom. *Project Joseph* wants to help people heal, so they can live their God-designed life! Great for small group or individual study. (Read an excerpt at the end of this book.)

Dream House: By Barry Bandara

Dream House is all about marriage and family. Barry Bandara has written an excellent book, using the blueprint of a house, to guide readers into developing God-pleasing marriages and family. *Dream House* takes its readers on a room-by-room tour of a well-designed home to illustrate the powerful principles of family and marriage laid out in God's Word. This is another great Overboard title, perfect for small groups. (Pastors, this is an excellent book to base a preaching series on. Order copies for your congregation and then preach a series following the outline of the book. Makes a great one-two punch!)

Extreme Mind Makeover: By Steve Etner

Steve has written a very compelling book that challenges readers to apply God's Word to their way of thinking. Steve points out that everyday actions come from every-moment thinking, so, if we want our actions to please God, we must start with God-pleasing thoughts. This book was forged out of Steve's personal journey and is a powerful tool filled with practical illustrations and loaded with Scripture. Learn to break bad habits and conquer sin with this book, which is perfect for counselors.

From Ruby Ridge to Freedom: The Sara Weaver Story (August, 2012)

On August 21st, 1992, the tragedy at Ruby Ridge in northern Idaho began, involving Randy Weaver and his family. During the standoff, 13-year-old Sam Weaver was shot and killed by federal agents, and Vicki Weaver, Randy's wife, was also killed by government snipers. After the 11 day siege had ended, and years after all the court cases had been concluded, the government essentially acknowledged egregious mistakes in its conduct with the Weaver family. And while financial settlement were made, the surviving Weavers had little healing. 16-year-old Sara Weaver was on Ruby Ridge the days her brother and mother were shot. She was there through it all, experiencing each terror through her teenage eyes.

Now, 20 years after the events on Ruby Ridge, Sara is telling the story of those days from her perspective. She is writing about the pain and heartache of those 11 nights on Ruby Ridge and how her life was forever changed. But she's also telling a different story, one few people have heard. She's telling the story of how a relationship with Jesus has made it possible for her to forgive the people who destroyed her childhood and took away her mom and brother. She is sharing a message of hope and healing, by sharing the process by which God gave it to her. Pick up a copy of *From Ruby Ridge to Freedom: The Sara Weaver Story* and be challenged to let God bring healing to your deepest heartache.

Overboard Ministries is growing, and we are on the look-out for more exciting titles. Be sure to check out our web site www.overboardministries.com often, for the latest Overboard titles. You can also follow us on facebook for up-to-the-minute information on our newest releases and projects.

About the Cover

Jan 31, 2012

The construction stripes on the top edge of the cover and the faded blueprint in the background are common threads to this series, symbolizing the main thrust of the series, that of (re)building or (re)constructing an individual, spiritually based on Scripture. The first book in this series, *Project Joseph,* focused on the rebuilding of the heart and mind of an individual who has experienced significant pain in his life. This second book in the series, *Project Nehemiah,* is about building — or rebuilding as the case may be — a truly remarkable life from something that may have once seemed ordinary, or even in shambles.

The looming shadow of a broken-down castle wall on the front and back cover signify the wreckage we are spiritually, emotionally, and physically as a result of sin. When an individual makes the proper choices, (re)construction can be made of the shambles of his life. The series of construction workers symbolizes the planning of the Architect, practical application of knowledge, physical effort, accountability, and the hard work that rebuilding a life can be.

But as we all know, in any construction project done properly, the resulting architecture is always worth the effort put into the building process. Even though the process can be gruelingly hard work, often requiring long periods of time, the shiny new building that results is a remarkable masterpiece of craftsmanship that provides shelter, warmth, fellowship, and opportunity for those who encounter it. The third book in the series, *Project Peter,* focuses on how to live the Overboard Life, *today* — creating opportunity through personal discipline.

Nate Horton
www.igprodesign.com

Project Joseph
Chapter 1, Preview

* * * * *

The Past lies upon the Present like a giant's dead body.
Nathaniel Hawthorne

ONE: PAIN IS EVERYWHERE

Many of us feel that our past is hovering above us, crashing down around us, lurking in the dark shadows waiting to pounce on us, or just attaching itself to our legs and dragging us down each and every day. In *The Neurotic's Notebook,* Mignon McLaughlin said it like this: "The past is strapped to our backs. We do not have to see it; we can always feel it." Naturally, our past has an incredibly profound impact on how we live in the present, and on what we'll do for God in the future.

All of us have seen pain. We've experienced pain. We've inflicted pain. We've seen different types of pain: physical, emotional, spiritual, mental and relational. Life is full of pain and no matter where we go or who we are with, we will all have pain in our lives — it's a natural consequence of living in a fallen world. Pain is everywhere.

While many authors have more personal experience in dealing with pain than I do, they often make two huge (and incorrect) assumptions about pain. The first is that pain can somehow be avoided. If we just surround ourselves with the right people, they say, if we put our kids in the right environment, build up tall enough walls, establish safe enough boundaries, and have enough faith, then we can go through life relatively pain-free. In fact, some take it a step further, saying that God doesn't even want His children to experience pain. So, according to them, when you are experiencing pain, God is punishing you until you come back to His truth. Once you do, He will again remove pain from your life until you stumble again.

Granted, there is a subtle half-truth at play here, but it is only half the truth. We can insulate ourselves from some pain. We can protect our families and loved ones from some heart ache, but to think we have total control over the pain that enters our lives is to put our own will over that of God's. Yes, sometimes God uses pain to get a hold of His children and yes, sometimes He uses pain as our earthly parents use pain in order to correct our bad behavior (Hebrews 12:7-11). Sometimes following God does lead to incredible blessing, temporarily free of pain. These are all partially possible. *Sometimes.*

The second common faulty assumption is that pain is so inevitable and so deeply rooted in us that the best we can do is merely cope with it, attempting to minimize its impact on our present life. We are urged to find the sources of pain when we can, and to cast blame on those guilty of the hurt. Then we are urged to run from circumstances that would have us repeat the offense or place ourselves back in harm's way. According to many writers on the subject of pain, it's not that God wants us to go through pain, but He allows it. It then becomes our job to unpack it for what we can, shift the blame for what we can't understand, and then ditch those experiences forever in our emotional garbage heap.

Again, there is a subtle half-truth involved in this concept of dealing with our pain, but again, it is only *half* the truth. It is possible to dispose of our pain (for a season), and often we can find others at the source of our pain (to some degree). But this method of dealing with our pain ignores *all* responsibility you or I might have for our pain. It assumes that any bad thing that has happened to us is to be dealt with and forgotten, and that it's not our fault. And yes, running from situations or people that are perennial pain inflicters is wise and even biblical — *sometimes.*

I believe there is a third option when it comes to pain. It's what I believe the Bible teaches in both description (examples from people's lives) and prescription (clear teaching). This third alternative, based on some core Scriptures, is this: God does not allow any pain to be wasted in our lives when we surrender it to Him.

In this option, pain is like any other part of life in that God is fully aware, He is fully in control, and He is giving us the freedom to make choices concerning our responses to life's painful circumstances. To embrace this view is to take away the blame of pain, to stop trying to live life devoid of pain, and to try to actually embrace it (yes, embrace it!) when it comes our way. In this view of pain, stuffing our past in the garbage disposal of the brain is not the answer. There's something grand to be learned, something powerful God wants us to grasp: God allows each heartache *for a reason*. This view does not allow us to live our lives avoiding or burying pain.

This option comes with two major assumptions:

1. **All pain is good pain when seen through the right lens.**
I'm not a masochist. I don't enjoy pain. In fact, I'm a bit soft when it comes to pain. However, you'll notice that I didn't say, "All pain is pleasurable" or "All pain is a good experience" or even that "All pain will be joyfully received once we get through it." The goodness of pain isn't found in the act of experiencing it, and what makes pain "bad" in our lives isn't the severity of the pain — it's the lens through which we are viewing the pain.

Before we move any further, it's important to establish a working definition of pain. In trying to create a definition I want to avoid being too narrow (by limiting heartache to a particular category: emotional, mental, physical, spiritual). I also am trying to avoid narrow parameters by not including the degree of pain in my definition. In other words, just because something is hurtful to me doesn't mean it has to be hurtful to you in order for both of us to agree that I'm in pain. You may ache over the loss of a beloved pet while someone else may simply return to the pet store to purchase a replacement. Both of those mistakes would leave some people out of the pain loop, implying that some live life free of pain.

In light of that, let's define pain as "anything contrary to ideal." That could be a lousy grade on a paper you studied hard for, a broken leg, a broken heart, or a car accident that results in the tragic loss of someone you loved. At one level or another, all of those are types of pain. This definition doesn't limit pain to a particular category and doesn't tell you how much something has to hurt before it can be categorized as pain.

I am blessed to be the father of three beautiful children. (Listen, pastors have kids for one main reason: Illustrations!) BJ — my middle child and oldest daughter — like me, has a very low pain threshold. Her concept of "ideal" involves princes and princesses and being waited on hand and foot. A butler and a maid aren't necessary, but certainly would be welcomed. Anything less than that is "pain" for her and will often be accompanied by angry words, pouty looks or fountains of tears. I love her dearly and you better believe she is Daddy's little girl, but Traci and I are constantly working with her to help her put her pain in perspective.

For example, her favorite meal has always been spaghetti. She's only eight right now, but this has been her favorite meal since she was two! One evening not too long ago, we visited some friends' house for dinner. The husband made spaghetti, to the joy and delight of my daughter…right up until the moment she tasted it. To her, the spaghetti tasted awful. The very moment those dangly noodles entered her mouth, her taste buds were offended, all of her joy was taken away and her life was filled with intense and immeasurable displeasure.

Our friend's spaghetti, in BJ's eyes, was less than ideal. She produced an ocean of big, hot tears like I did at her age when my favorite cowboy hat was carelessly launched from my head into a mud puddle...oh, the agony! Through the lens of my daughter's perspective, this man had perpetrated a crime against humanity, and the offender (sorry, Chad) ought to be punished severely — skinning would not be too harsh!

Now look at this circumstance again through the lens of her father. Dad — who is trying to teach his daughter to value people over food, and trying to help her understand what it means to be gracious in all circumstances — thinks that this pain is good for her. It allows the issues of selfishness and control to come right to the surface so that they can be discussed, and growth can occur. He's convinced that what his daughter sees as a world-changing trauma might be yet another talking point to help her see her pain through a different lens. (He's also totally humiliated, which is another type of pain entirely!) The same pain viewed through different lenses allows us to see either an appalling culinary crime against humanity or an opportunity for growth. My daughter *could choose* a different lens through which to view this pain.

Let's take this illustration even further by viewing this agony through the lens of someone living in a nation with inadequate food. How would they view my daughter's "pain" at the dinner table? As BJ's father, I see a growth opportunity. If I were a starving child I would see a survival opportunity — a meal that gives me another day of life. Same pain, different lens.

Again, I stress that I am not saying that all pain is enjoyable, pleasurable or even desirable. I'm simply stating the first assumption of this third view of pain: All pain is good pain when viewed through the right lens.

2. **I do not have to live in victimhood with my pain.**

This assumption is the one that gets personal and may have some of you already wishing you hadn't purchased this book.

Hang in there with me, because I believe this concept may have the most significant impact on how many of us view our pain.

By definition, a victim is merely someone who has been subjected to some negative experience which they had not planned on, or had intended to avoid. A victim of a car crash doesn't usually want to get into an accident any more than a victim of a financial scam wants to have all their money taken away. Regardless of the circumstances of the guy involved in the accident or the woman swindled out of her life savings, neither sought their particular painful outcome. Both are, by definition, victims. Simply put, to be a victim means to experience something in your life that isn't ideal — i.e., pain.

In today's culture, however, many victims live in "victimhood." This word has become synonymous with "I deserve better." Worse than that, a notion has developed that says someone else needs to step in and rectify your painful situation when you are in victimhood, and rectify it NOW! In the news lately, we've seen repeated instances of victimhood in relation to mortgages. When banks fall "victim" to patrons bailing out on their home loans, they live in victimhood, waiting in line until the government bails *them* out. Why? Because they think they deserve better than to have to pay for over-indebted consumers who took loans they couldn't afford.

Likewise, when home owners find themselves in circumstances which leave them unable to pay their monthly mortgage payment — because they took out more than they could afford or they fell on hard times — and the bank has the gall to ask them to make good on their monthly commitments, they are "victims" of bad lending practices. Many choose to live in this perceived victimhood, waiting in line for the government to bail them out. Why? Because they shouldn't even have been given the chance to borrow money they couldn't afford to repay. They languish in victimhood, waiting for someone to make things right. You see, in victimhood people are powerless, God is quiet, slow or even cruel, and life is full of blame. In victimhood I'm not responsible for my choices, and, worst of all, there is nothing I can do to remedy my current situation.

Don't get me wrong, there are lots of reasons — and many of them incredibly painful — for falling behind in a mortgage or becoming overextended. My wife and I have often felt the financial pinch (more like the financial vice grip of death!) in our personal resources. Yet regardless of the reasons, I still have a choice about whether or not to live in victimhood.

When our youngest daughter was born, Traci and I got a first-hand glimpse into the choices we can make regarding the pain of financial pressure. Celina was due January 20th but decided to make an early appearance to cash in on the Christmas gift-giving season, instead of having to wait another year to experience holiday fun. So we were delighted, and a little nervous, to head to the hospital on December 20th when Traci said, "It's time." Being born 35 days early gave CJ the "preemie" tag and left her with a few issues, including under-developed lungs. Three days after taking her home, we returned to the hospital, and CJ spent 48 hours in the NICU (intensive care for babies) before she got to come home in time for New Years.

Less than four weeks after arriving home, she began to have some breathing issues, and, on a follow-up doctor's appointment, my wife was instructed to head directly to the ER to have CJ admitted. We spent another two or three nights of praying and fretting as Celina was put back on a ventilator while we waited for her health to change. Thankfully, God provided a top-notch pediatrician and incredible nursing staff so that we took her home and haven't had a return trip since!

Two weeks after CJ's stay, we got a bill from the hospital. After insurance had paid all they were going to pay, we owed the hospital over $10,000. I offered to give them one of my arms as payback, but apparently that's just an expression and not an actual accepted form of payment. So we started negotiating fees, and tried to figure out how on earth we would pay for this beautiful child.

Several more weeks passed and we received another bill. It too was over $10,000 and actually was a few hundred dollars higher than the first bill. I called the hospital to ask why they had added new costs to the existing invoice, only to discover that we were being billed for Celina's second visit. Until that day, I didn't know that insurance premiums and deductibles were based on the calendar year. Since CJ returned to the hospital *after* January 1st, we had to repay our deductibles and our insurance only covered a certain percentage of her second stay. If she had gone back before January 1st, insurance would have covered over 80%.

The two bills totaled well over $20,000, and we were instantly feeling the intense pain and pressure of financial heartache. Regardless of the source of our pain, we had to make a choice about how we were going to deal with it.

All of us are going to make bad decisions in our lives. All of us are going to be affected by someone else's bad decision. All of us will feel the crunch of situations over which we have no control; in other words, all of us are going to be "victims" in the basic sense of the word. However, it's those people who choose not to remain in victimhood who do incredible things for God and inspire others to live with excellence. It is the people who stick out horrible marriages with love, endure cancer with courage, face down workplace opposition with truth and grace, and forgive their abusive relatives with mercy who rise up to be what God intended them to be — who God MADE them to be!

Welcome to the journey

Throughout this book we will be taking a journey alongside one of the Bible's great men of faith. This man suffered tremendously. Pain was inflicted on him by his own decisions, from brothers, from parents, from employers, from friends and seemingly from God Himself. This guy went through a span of years that I wouldn't wish on my worst enemy! Yet he found a way to keep seeing pain through God's lens and to avoid the temptation of living in victimhood.

As we walk through his story, you will have the opportunity to take some of your hurt from the past and begin the process of coping and healing. I believe some of you will also take some past pain and deal with it once and for all, the way God wants you to.

I don't know what pain you've gone through. Though I've experienced deep heartache and sorrow, I won't pretend that I've experienced an incredibly difficult life up to this point. But pain is no respecter of persons. Although we try to compare or rate our difficult experiences with someone else's, trying to measure how much hurt someone should feel in any given circumstance is nearly impossible. Worse than that, it is unproductive and leads back to neglecting our personal responsibility. Instead, what we can do is free ourselves from the chains of victimhood and discover what it's like to live free from the bondage of pain. Not a life free from pain, but free from the enslavement we place ourselves under when we let pain and hurt and heartache and bitterness rule our lives.

I hope you will take advantage of the "homework" section at the end of each chapter. These assignments will help you articulate and apply the principles from this book to your specific situation. The more time you take to be thorough in working through those assignments, the more effective this book will be for you.

Welcome to the journey, and may God give you what only He can as you endeavor to leave your brokenness with Him:

Come to me, all you who are weary and burdened,
and I will give you rest. — Matthew 11:28

Homework

Over the next few chapters we are going to unpack the following verses. Sometimes these verses have been totally misused and abused even by well-meaning Christians. Sometimes they've just been ripped out of context and stripped of their power. We'll get to that. Today, however, just read them and spend some time thinking about each one. Think about how these passages could free you from your own pain, and spend some time talking to God. Maybe you need to confess faithlessness before Him. Maybe you need to cry out for comfort. Maybe you just need to reaffirm your faith in His plan. Whatever it is, talk to Him after you've spent some time reflecting on His Word.

And we know that in all things God works for the good of those who love Him, who have been called according to His purpose. — Romans 8:28

Praise be to the God and Father of our Lord Jesus Christ, the Father of compassion and the God of all comfort, who comforts us in all our troubles, so that we can comfort those in any trouble with the comfort we ourselves have received from God. — 2 Corinthians 1:3-4

Consider it pure joy, my brothers, whenever you face trials of many kinds, because you know that the testing of your faith develops perseverance. Perseverance must finish its work so that you may be mature and complete, not lacking anything. — James 1:2-4

* * * * *